▶ Defining Democracy in a Digital Age

DOI: 10.1057/9781137496195.0001

Other Palgrave Pivot titles

DOI: 10.1057/9781137496195.0001

palgrave▶pivot

Defining Democracy in a Digital Age: Political Support on Social Media

Barend Lutz
Digital Media Manager and Political Risk Analyst, Red24, South Africa

and

Pierre du Toit
Professor, Department of Political Science, University of Stellenbosch, South Africa

DOI: 10.1057/9781137496195.0001

First published 2014 by
PALGRAVE MACMILLAN

Palgrave Macmillan in the UK is an imprint of Macmillan Publishers Limited, registered in England, company number 785998, of Houndmills, Basingstoke, Hampshire RG21 6XS.

Palgrave Macmillan in the US is a division of St Martin's Press LLC, 175 Fifth Avenue, New York, NY 10010.

Palgrave Macmillan is the global academic imprint of the above companies and has companies and representatives throughout the world.

Palgrave® and Macmillan® are registered trademarks in the United States, the United Kingdom, Europe and other countries.

ISBN: 978–1–137–49620–1 EPUB
ISBN: 978–1–137–49619–5 PDF
ISBN: 978–1–137–49618–8 Hardback

A catalogue record for this book is available from the British Library.

A catalog record for this book is available from the Library of Congress.

www.palgrave.com/pivot

DOI: 10.1057/9781137496195

Contents

DOI: 10.1057/9781137496195.0001

DOI: 10.1057/9781137496195.0001

List of Figures

DOI: 10.1057/9781137496195.0002

List of Tables

Acknowledgements

Pierre du Toit would like to thank South Africa's National Research Foundation (NRF) for financial assistance received for this project through grant no. IFR2008051600007, as well as the financial support received from Stellenbosch University.

Barend Lutz would like to express the deepest appreciation to Professor Gert-Jan van Rooyen and Dr. Herman Engelbrecht, the MIH Media Lab and Naspers, who not only financed the thesis that forms the backbone to this book, but also provided the stimulating working environment.

We both would like to extend our thanks to Kathleen Wood for her expert copy-editing of the manuscript in South Africa.

We would like to record our appreciation for the permission received to quote from published works. These are from Benedict Anderson's *Imagined Communities. Reflections on the Origins and Spread of Nationalism* (revised edition, 2006); from Manuel Castells's *Networks of Outrage and Hope. Social Movements in the Internet Age* (2011); and from Frank Dikötter's *The Tragedy of Liberation. A History of the Chinese Revolution 1945–57* (2013), © Frank Dikötter, 'The Tragedy of Liberation'. Every effort has been made to trace all copyright holders, but if any have been inadvertently overlooked, the publisher will be pleased to make the necessary arrangements at the first opportunity.

DOI: 10.1057/9781137496195.0004

Personal acknowledgements

Barend would like to express his heartfelt gratitude towards everyone that supported him during the writing of this book. He would like to start by showing his most humble gratitude to the Lord for giving him the strength, courage and ability to complete this book. To Professor du Toit, his inspiring supervisor and co-author, who motivated and continuously guided his work, he extends his profound gratitude. Also to Dr. Derica Lambrechts who, with her keen logical approach, provided truly helpful insight. Next, to Prof. Anthony Leysens and the Political Science Department for taking such an interest in his work and allowing him to represent the department. Barend would then like to extend copious amounts of thanks to his family, who supported him throughout his life and his studies; specific appreciation goes out to his brother, Frederick, who provided econometrical expertise in support of this book. Last, but far from least, he would like to thank Marina for her continuous support, inspiration and editorial help.

Pierre du Toit gladly acknowledges the contribution made by Leon du Toit, who alerted us to the concept of imagined communities, key to the overall coherence of what we try to convey in this book.

DOI: 10.1057/9781137496195.0004

List of Abbreviations

GCDD	Ghana Centre for Democratic Development
GDELT	Global Dataset of Events, Location and Tone
HTTP	Hypertext Transfer Protocol
ICT	information and communications technology
IDASA	Institute for Democracy in South Africa
LTP	long-term potentiation
NLP	natural language processing
OWSM	Occupy Wall Street Movement
PPACA	Patient Protection and Affordable Care Act
VOTP	Voice of the People
WEF	World Economic Forum
WVS	World Values Survey

DOI: 10.1057/9781137496195.0005

1
Democracy in the New Digital Age

Abstract: *Chapter 1 introduces the two main intertwined themes of the book. Our first theme joins up with a long list of analysts who note the current doubts about the viability of democracy as a system of rule. The second follows from that. If democracy is to be secured in the twenty-first century, then its practices and institutions will have to be compatible with the communications technology of the Internet, especially social media, which has already shown its power as an instrument of political mobilisation in the Arab Spring revolutions in Tunisia and Egypt, along with the Occupy Wall Street. But democratic durability also needs forces of social cohesion, and here social media, in our view, can also be decisively influential. We conclude by presenting the central question addressed in the book: can digital media, including social media, contribute to creating new, durable imagined communities favourable to the re-construction of the social base of democracies?*

Keywords: digital social media; imagined communities; social requisites of democracy

Lutz, Barend and Pierre du Toit. *Defining Democracy in a Digital Age: Political Support on Social Media.* Basingstoke: Palgrave Macmillan, 2014. DOI: 10.1057/9781137496195.0006.

Two intertwined themes are elaborated in this book. The first is the concern with democracy as a system of government. With the start of the Third Wave of democratisation in Portugal in 1974, and especially with the impetus provided by the end of the Cold War in 1989, optimism peaked about the prospects of extending this type of regime to more and more societies hitherto under authoritarian rule of some or other type. By the end of the century, however, concern about a Third Reverse Wave appeared to be taking shape. It was with this wave that doubts about the global prospects of democracy began to surface.

The Global Financial Crisis, which took off in 2008 in the United States and impacted rapidly on the global economy, added another measure of doubt about democracy. This time the concern was not just about the viability of democracies at the edges of the democratic zone in the developing world, but also about the quality of democracies at the centre – such as the United States and some members of the Eurozone – and especially about the economic base of these democracies. Yet another layer of doubt was added by the so-called Arab Spring, which started with the overthrow of autocratic rules in Tunisia and Egypt in 2011, and was followed by Libya shortly after. Initially it was thought by many that another wave of democratisation was sweeping the Arab world, hence the notion of 'Spring'. Yet, in none of the three Arab states mentioned earlier has democracy been stabilised, nor has it spread elsewhere into the Arab world with success.

These three distinct historical episodes and their concerns about democracy as a system of rule do not stand alone. They form part of a thread of thought that goes far back into the history of democracy and the history of thought about the viability of democracy. What makes this 'politics of doubt' in the twenty-first century different from anything that existed before is the increasingly active role played by the new Internet-based communications technologies.

This leads to the second theme of this book. Communications technologies, such as the plethora of social media platforms available, stand at the apex of a wave of technological innovation that has been compared to that of the Industrial Revolution. Driving this wave is the exponential increase in computing power, usually expressed in what is now called 'Moore's Law'. This is the observation made by Gordon Moore, co-founder of Intel, which states that the number of transistors that could be fitted onto a computer chip has doubled every 18 months from the time that the chip was invented up to the time of his writing in 1965.[1] This rapid growth has not only led to multifaceted changes in the established capitalist societies, but also in the developing world. Computer-driven machines are increasingly taking over mostly middle-class jobs, with concomitant declines in job security and lower employment levels. These destabilising changes were not limited to the economic base of established democracies, but also spread to the social base to undermine the social cohesion democracies need to function as stable and durable regimes. A screen culture has become omnipresent in those societies with saturation levels of penetration by the Internet. Such a culture affects social life in a fundamental way as it changes how people communicate and otherwise engage with one another. Digital social media, with Facebook, WeChat, Twitter and YouTube as leading examples, have become major global channels of communication, with ramifications for established democracies and their social bases – some positive, others disruptive.

One of the ways in which social media enhances democratic participation is through the potential global connectivity of this technology. Individuals also gain almost complete control over the content of the statements they release on the Internet. Individual self-expression, a key component of democratic participation, is therefore presented into the public space more efficiently than ever before. It should be noted, however, that this capacity is a double-edged sword as it can also work to the detriment of democracy. There is, as yet, no effective way of converting such articulate mass self-expression by individuals into coherent forms that can mesh with established democratic institutions to serve as effective demands capable of shaping public policies. In short, these expressions lack structure: they have yet to be ordered into categories and have yet to be ranked in order of preference. Until such structure is attained, it is argued, throughout this book, that social media is likely to continue to inhibit the maintenance of social cohesion in these societies.

The aim here is to examine the impact of information and communications technology (ICT) on the social base of democracies by using a conceptual framework that is located within political science rather than the related fields of communication studies and the sociology of social movements. The social requisites of democracy, as presented in the authoritative political science literature from the late 1950s onwards, have been referenced by the authors of this study to consider the impact of these technologies on society. This means that when the political impact

DOI: 10.1057/9781137496195.0006

of social media is interpreted, the key concepts from political systems analyses are used, such as demand generation and the conversion processes of interest articulation and interest aggregation. When the impact of these technologies on the social cohesion of democracies is interpreted, Benedict Anderson's concept of imagined communities[2] is drawn on, as well as the core concepts of a Civic Culture and of social capital. From this conceptual framework the following question is presented: can digital media, including social media, contribute to creating new, durable imagined communities favourable to the re-construction of the social base of democracies?

The approach here to answering this question is to address this lack of structure. This is done by presenting original data analysis methods with which a quantitative sentiment analysis is conducted from a large dataset from Twitter. With this it will be demonstrated that sentiment about a specific issue can be aggregated into categories – a crucial first step in creating structure.

Today there is an explosive increase in online data: blogs, social networks, web pages, digitised books and articles, and many other forms of electronic documents – all of which mean that there is much more information available. At the World Economic Forum (WEF) meeting in Davos, Switzerland, in January 2012, 'Big Data'[3] was heralded as a new type of valuable economic asset.[4] The sentiment rife in the academic and business world alike is that Big Data and the rapidly advancing ICT using Big Data can and will 'open the door to a new approach to understanding the world and making decisions'.[5] However, this rise in the quantity of information necessitates more efficient, automated methods of data analysis.

Within the field of computer science there are already a number of automated content-analysis applications which are well-suited for computer science purposes. We, as authors, believe, along with others such as Hopkins and King before us, that these applications can and should be adapted to fit social sciences better.[6] In this study, this function of a content-analysis programme will be paramount as it will be used to highlight the information that is relevant to the chosen topic of democracy.

Within blogs and microblogs (such as Twitter) a large number of people are voicing their opinions on various issues. One could view these opinions as visible public expressions of opinion or interest articulation, which might be more valuable to political scientists than attitudes and

DOI: 10.1057/9781137496195.0006

non-attitudes expressed in traditional survey responses.[7] Not all scholars, however, agree with the opinion that these visible expressions of opinion are more valuable than the poll data. For instance, in a critical review of Ginsberg's book *The Captive Public: How Mass Opinion Promotes State Power*,[8] Smith highlights some of the problems such as over-emphasised opinions of certain actors or strong views and the inability to determine whether an opinion comes from a knowledgeable person. With regard to this discussion on the preference of polling or visible expression methods of measuring public opinion, it is important to remember that neither of these techniques is infallible. It is, however, encouraging to see that, as O'Connor et al. noted: '[E]xpensive and time-intensive polling can be supplemented or supplanted with the simple-to-gather text data that are generated from online social networking'.[9]

The O'Connor et al. study focussed on comparing public opinion measured from polls with sentiment measured from text. They correlated sentiments gathered from Twitter during 2008–2009 with traditional approval polling and consumer-confidence polling results for the same period. Using this Twitter data, their findings show that, even with a relatively simple sentiment detector, the results are comparable to much more time-intensive (and expensive) polling methods.

This book adds to the new methods of measuring social realities which are constantly being developed. The focus, however, is on Twitter, the second biggest online social network, after Facebook, which contains a mass of user-generated data from around the globe. By taking advantage of specific technological advancements in the field of automated content and sentiment analysis, it might be possible to gain a deeper understanding of certain important aspects of political and social life. Within the academic field of political culture, there exists the belief that the functioning and persistence of democracy and democratic institutions is integrally linked with dominant mass tendencies in individual-level attitudes and value orientations.[10] What these studies show is that what people think about democracy and democratic institutions is important to the functioning of democracy as a political system of governance.

The rationale for the link between opinions of citizens and the functioning of a democracy is based on the idea of a public sphere. This idea will be further elaborated, but in brief it refers to a physical or virtual space where the public can meet to discuss, debate and deliberate on public affairs. The public sphere lies between state and society and is an essential component of socio-political organisation. It provides a form of

DOI: 10.1057/9781137496195.0006

legitimacy and accountability to a government and a space for citizens to participate in public affairs.[11]

The social media site, Twitter, will be examined as a type of public sphere in this study. Within this public sphere, global citizens are constantly discussing a multitude of issues. One of these issues that receive constant discussion on Twitter is democracy. If one can measure public expressions on democracy, one could, in theory, be able to gain deeper insights into the health of democracy. There are, however, various ways in which public expressions on democracy can be gauged, as will be shown in Chapter 2. In the past, most studies that attempted to measure expressions or opinions about democracy have used surveys consisting of rigid, standardised questionnaires. The rationale of this book is to develop the methodology for measuring public expressions on democracy from Twitter which will be built upon, tested and expressed through a descriptive analysis of expressions (Tweets) on democracy from Twitter for the period of 1 May to 31 July 2012.

In selecting the issue to be analysed, one returns to the first concern: the persistent question about the global support for democracy as a system of rule. The Tweets that will be examined are all about democracy, but since many bear on both positive and negative expressions on democracy, the overall sentiment will be analysed. This measurement will then be compared with the strengths and weaknesses of public opinion surveys, the pre-eminent instruments of measuring public opinion up to the present time.

As the process is an ongoing one, with no clear cut-off point, an assessment of the overall impact of the computer-driven technological revolution on democracy and its social and economic base is not yet possible. Instead, one can draw on other authors who dare to envisage aspects of future society and the role of Internet-based technology in shaping the prospects of democracy in such an age. With this one can consider the social requisites for the creation of new, stable imagined communities in such an age, and of the properties of the information required to nurture such communities. One can then conclude by reflecting on the extent to which this data analysis methodology has already contributed to shaping information in such a way, and what will be needed from new software that builds on what is presented here.

The authors believe that the world is on the brink of realising the full potential of Big Data analysis. Therefore, this introductory study about measuring expressions on democracy with Twitter aims to open

DOI: 10.1057/9781137496195.0006

up the field for future research on measuring public expressions from social media sites. One is thus able to draw valuable conclusions from this study and provide insights that can be of benefit to future research in the field of automated content analysis. It should be noted that the technology used in this study is still in its infancy but is growing rapidly. As technological advancements improve in natural language processing (NLP), artificial intelligence, automated content analysis and machine learning, the methods described in this study will also improve.

The chapter outlines are summarised as follows. In Chapter 2 an over-view is provided of the core theoretical approaches to democratic stability, as elaborated in the second half of the twentieth century. This serves as a conceptual framework for making sense of the social and political impact of the current wave of technological innovation on established democracies. A start is made with the two benchmark criteria of democracy – citizen effectiveness and system capacity – as set by Robert Dahl and Edward Tufte.[12] In this study, the concern is with the former criterion only. The then (mid-twentieth century) authoritative arguments are outlined about how citizen effectiveness is attained in modern democracies through an appropriate political culture (the Civic Culture), social cohesion (through social capital) and political cohesion (through imagined communities in the form of national identities) as shaped by the then prevailing communication technologies (mostly print media). These conditions for democracy are then contrasted with those of mass societies – also as understood in the mid-twentieth century – which present the conditions for mobilising people into totalitarian regimes.

In the latter part of Chapter 2, some of the major challenges to the established wisdom about the social and economic conditions (what is referred to here as the social base) for democracy are presented. The first is the so-called transition paradigm, a school of thought which promotes the idea that democracy could prosper without the social preconditions identified by earlier theorists. The second is found in empirical studies, mostly from the United States, that show that social capital was declining by the latter part of the twentieth century and that this was a function of new technology: first television and then the Internet (the latter to be discussed in Chapter 4). This implied that the 'new economy' of advanced capitalism was actually eroding the social base of democracy as we knew it then.

Chapter 3 is divided into four broad sections. Firstly, the value of measuring expressions on democracy is briefly examined. Traditional

DOI: 10.1057/9781137496195.0006

literature on the value of public opinions to the democratic consolidation and functioning of democracies is discussed in this section. Secondly, an examination of traditional methods of measuring expressions on democracy can be found. Thirdly, Twitter is examined as a new form of the Habermasian public sphere. Highlighted here is how Twitter can be seen as a place of mass online gathering and where public opinions are created. Finally, a section on novel emerging methods of measuring public expressions from online sources follows. This section specifically looks at a number of recent studies which have used Twitter to gauge public expressions. The broad aim of this chapter is to show the importance of measuring expressions and opinions on democracy; to show how this measurement has been done up to now; and finally, to illustrate novel methods – such as the method developed in this book – that might lead to an alternative way of measurement. This is not to claim that this method will replace traditional methods of measuring expressions on democracy; but it is believed that it could supplement and enhance the data gathered using traditional methods.

Chapter 4 can be seen as a practical guide and example of using this novel methodology of measuring democracy on Twitter. The broad goal of this chapter is to develop, run and provide the results of the specific research procedures (operations) that will result in empirical observations for measuring public expressions on democracy from Twitter. This analysis attempts to show the extent to which one can measure public expressions on democracy from interest-articulated sentiments gathered from a sample of Tweets, processed with content-analysis and sentiment-analysis software. In layman's terms, it is an attempt to show how accurate the measurement of democracy on Twitter is. Further, the commercial data processing platform selected for analysis is examined.[13] The rationale for the choice and the functioning of this platform – with its limitations – is also expressed.

The second section of this chapter contains the results of the measurement of public expressions on democracy from interest-articulated sentiments gathered from a sample of Tweets, processed with content-analysis and sentiment-analysis software. This section specifically relates measuring public expressions on democracy from the period 1 May to 31 July 2012.

The third section of this chapter delves deeper into the accuracy of content-analysis and sentiment-analysis software used in measuring public expressions on democracy. This section contains a manual

DOI: 10.1057/9781137496195.0006

assessment of the classification results made by the researchers of the commercial data processing platform.

Following these three sections, a section on the broad relevance of these findings can be found. There are a number of other interesting findings that have emerged out of this study which will also be briefly examined. The authors believe that this study has the potential to open up the field of automated measurement of public expressions from online textual data. The final section, therefore, examines potential routes that future research might take within this novel field.

In Chapter 5, the current and conceivable future impact that Internet-based technology can have on the social base required by democracies is considered. Current impacts are dramatically demonstrated in the social movements of the Arab Spring, with Tunisia and Egypt presented as the leading examples. The brief surge of the Occupy Wall Street Movement replicated in many cities throughout the world is also notable, both for its global manifestation and for its fleeting existence on the ground. The authors conclude that these examples demonstrate that social media holds huge promise for democracy in the capacity of interest articulation, but falls short with respect to interest aggregation. The section closes by outlining what we consider to be the necessary attributes of the properties of the information needed to rebuild imagined communities in the Digital Age, and we argue that the methodology demonstrated in this book already goes some way into constructing these attributes.

The next section of this chapter provides an overview of the likely future impact of the technology of the new Digital Age. These are of necessity of a speculative nature, and in presenting strongly contrasting views we aim to open the field of debate as wide as possible. A view on the impact of these technologies on personal identity is presented from the field of neuroscience, with an opposing perspective from the profession of computer-based gaming. We find links between propositions that arise from these contrasting views to our previous analyses about the social base for democracies. These include arguments relating to the social isolation of individuals (with its impact on social capital formation and on social cohesion) to the world of politics and also to that of the mass society that serves as the social base for totalitarian regimes.

Further implications for democracy are considered in a perspective on a future America with a radically changed social base, in which politics and society are dominated by a cognitive elite, and in which the middle class has withered. This section concludes with an assessment by an

DOI: 10.1057/9781137496195.0006

authoritative futurist of some of the confident predictions made about the impact of the Internet some years ago, and how inaccurate some of them have proved to be.[14] The author of this assessment then makes some revised predictions, and we embed our study with its findings and the implications we draw from it into this set of revised forecasts.

Notes

1   J.J. Hughes (2008) 'Millennial Tendencies in Responses to Apocalyptic Threats', in N. Bostrom and M.M. Cirkovic (eds), *Global Catastrophic Risks* (Oxford: Oxford University Press), p. 79.

2   B. Anderson (2006) *Imagined Communities. Reflections on the Origin and Spread of Nationalism,* revised edn (New York: Verso).

3   Big Data refers to the analysis of massive data sets (today even terabytes, petabytes and exabytes in size) which require exceptional technologies in order to be processed within reasonable time. The analysis of data gathered from social media sites such as Twitter can be seen as Big Data.

4   WEF (2012) *Big Data, Big Impact: New Possibilities for International Development.* World Economic Forum: Vital Wave Consulting. (Online, available at: http://www3.weforum.org/docs).

5   S. Lohr (2012) The Age of Big Data, *New York Times* (Online, available at: http://www.nytimes.com/2012/02/12).

6   D.J. Hopkins and G. King (2010) 'A Method of Automated Nonparametric Content Analysis for Social Science', *American Journal of Political Science,* 54(1), 229–247, at 229.

7   Hopkins and King, 'A Method of Automated Nonparametric Content Analysis', 231; B. Ginsberg (1986) *The Captive Public: How Mass Opinion Promotes State Power* (New York: Basic Books).

8   T.W. Smith, (1987) 'Book Review: The Captive Public: How Mass Opinion Promotes State Power', *American Journal of Sociology,* 93(2), 520–522.

9   B. O'Connor, R. Balasubramanyan, B. Routledge and N. Smith (2010) 'From Tweets to Polls: Linking Text Sentiment to Public Opinion Time Series', in *Proceedings of ICWSM*: Carnegie Mellon University.

10 D. Lerner (1958) *The Passing of Traditional Society: Modernization in the Middle East* (New York: Free Press); G.A. Almond and S. Verba (1963) *The Civic Culture: Political Attitudes and Democracy in Five Nations* (Boston: Little, Brown and Company); H. Eckstein (1966) *Division and Cohesion in Democracy: A Study of Norway* (Princeton: Princeton University Press); R. Inglehart and C. Welzel (2005) *Modernization, Cultural Change and Democracy: The Human Development Sequence* (Cambridge: Cambridge University Press).

DOI: 10.1057/9781137496195.0006

11   M. Castells (2008) 'The New Public Sphere: Global Civil Society, Communication Networks and Global Governance', *The Annals of the American Academy of Political and Social Science*, 616, 78–94.

12   R.A. Dahl and E.R. Tufte (1973) *Size and Democracy* (Stanford, CA: Stanford University Press).

13   This commercial firm declined to be named, but allowed us to use the results of the research undertaken by them.

14   K. Albrecht (2014) 'The Information Revolution's Broken Promises', *The Futurist*, 48(2). http://www.wfs.org/futurist/2014-issues-futurist/march-april-2014-vol-48-no-2.

DOI: 10.1057/9781137496195.0006

2

Twentieth-Century Democracy and Its Social Base

Abstract: *We start with the two benchmark criteria of democracy set by Robert Dahl and Edward Tufte, those of citizen effectiveness and of system capacity. We outline the then (mid-twentieth century) authoritative arguments about how citizen effectiveness is attained in modern democracies through an appropriate political culture (the civic culture), social cohesion (through social capital) and political cohesion (through imagined communities in the form of national identities) as shaped by the then prevailing communication technologies (mostly print media). These conditions for democracy are then contrasted with those of mass societies, the conditions for mobilising people into totalitarian regimes. In the latter part of the chapter we present two of the major challenges to the established wisdom about the social and economic conditions (what we refer to here as the social base) for democracy. The first is the so-called transition paradigm; the second is a function of yet new technology, first television and then the Internet.*

Keywords: atomisation; citizen effectiveness; civic culture; imagined communities; mass society; social capital; social cohesion; system capacity; transition paradigm

Lutz, Barend and Pierre du Toit. *Defining Democracy in a Digital Age: Political Support on Social Media.* Basingstoke: Palgrave Macmillan, 2014. DOI: 10.1057/9781137496195.0007.

DOI: 10.1057/9781137496195.0007

The evolving dynamics of modern democracies have been continuously shaped by technological and institutional innovations, by the values and beliefs found in the political culture of societies and by the factor of size. The Age of Modernity which took off in Europe by the late fifteenth century was said to have led this process with three technological innovations (all of which originated elsewhere): gunpowder, oceanic navigation and the printing press.[1] The major institutional innovation that emerged from the Middle Ages was that of Representative Assemblies.[2] Modern democracies benefited directly from one of these innovations – the technology of the printing press – invented in Europe in 1454 (and much earlier in China), which allowed ever larger populations of citizens to be drawn into political society. The political cultures that developed in the durable democracies of the twentieth century built on notions about, *inter alia*, the identity of the political society, shaped primarily by the ideology of nationalism; by the institutional framework of the nation(al)-state; and by the civic and political virtues captured in the evolving liberal-democratic human rights doctrines.

This chapter's focus is to consider the impact of the continuing major technological innovations on this era – that of the printing press and television – on the social requisites of democracy and on the political cultures of contemporary democratic societies. This begins with an overview of the development of the social base and attendant political culture of modern, established democracies from the mid-twentieth century onwards, as conceptualised and interpreted by some leading scholars. The concept of the Civic Culture threads through this overview, as it offers a conceptual vantage point for describing the destabilising impact of new communications technology on the Civic Culture and on its social base, with the potential implications for the viability of these democracies. At the conclusion of this overview, the following question is presented: Can digital media, including social media, contribute to creating new and durable imagined communities favourable to the reconstruction of the social base of these democracies?

The civic culture

It has been argued that, irrespective of size, the ideal democracy should meet the following two criteria: that of citizen effectiveness (where 'citizens acting responsibly and competently fully control the decisions of

DOI: 10.1057/9781137496195.0007

the polity') and that of system capacity (where 'the polity has the capacity to respond fully to the collective preferences of its citizens').[3]

The classical tradition, defined and upheld by Greek philosophers, argued that unit size is important in meeting these criteria and that smaller units are preferable over larger ones. Plato, hardly a democrat, arrived at an optimal number of 5,040 citizens (heads of households) per democratic unit. At this size, he argued, all citizens would know one another. Aristotle, without setting a numerical limit, also argued for smallness, roughly the number of people who could assemble within the range of a single unamplified human voice.[4] In such units citizens are effective because they can, by virtue of size, participate directly in decision-making. In addition, if such small democratic units are to respond fully to the decisions made by citizens, they need to be fully autonomous or even sovereign from other political entities. The Greek city-state, in the classical view, supposedly met these criteria. Yet Athens, the pre-eminent Greek city-state, at its zenith (432 BC) comprised 215,000–300,000 inhabitants, with citizens numbering about 30,000–45,000 – far above the numbers set by these philosophers.[5]

In the modern era, the requirements for meeting these criteria had to be revised substantially with the relocation of democratic units into larger regimes embedded within national states which are, in turn, units within a global state-system. Within this system of states, no unit other than the national state could have the capacity to respond fully to democratically expressed preferences, and thus only the national state could be fully autonomous, or sovereign. Yet citizen effectiveness is difficult to attain through direct democracy at the unit size of the national state. What remains for citizens is to participate indirectly, mostly through electing representatives to assemblies within which public policies are made.[6] The likelihood also arises of trade-offs between the achievement of both these two criteria at this level. At higher levels of citizen participation in democratic units of this large size, for instance, citizen effectiveness may well still be achieved but without the result of necessarily correspondingly higher levels of system capacity. The classic instance would be one of citizens effectively demanding public goods that exceed the capacity of the political economy of the democratic unit to produce.

Citizen effectiveness

The social base of effective citizen participation in the established democracies of the mid-twentieth century has been illuminated in a

DOI: 10.1057/9781137496195.0007

number of classic empirical studies. These studies have focussed on the attributes of the political culture of mature and stable democracies, such as: (i) the political culture of the society; (ii) the importance of social cohesion at the micro level; and (iii) of political cohesion at the national level. Each of these aspects of an effective democratic citizenry will be presented briefly in this chapter.

Political culture

A pioneering work in describing the features of the political culture of the leading established, legitimate and prosperous democracies of the mid-twentieth century is Almond and Verba's *The Civic Culture. Political Attitudes and Democracy in Five Nations.*[7] The book is a comparative study of Mexico, Italy, West Germany, the United Kingdom and the United States, with data taken from opinion surveys conducted in the late 1950s and early 1960s. The authors identify what they call a 'Civic Culture', which is, at its core, a participant political culture with citizens positively orientated to making demands on the political system and also intent on responding to government policies. This political culture also contains lesser elements of a subject political culture, typified by citizens who affec-tively judge their political system, either liking or disliking it, but with a low, even passive orientation to doing something about it in the public space in terms of democratic political participation. Some remnants of a parochial political culture are also found, where few demands are made, and citizens expect little, if anything, from the political system. There are also elements of an individualist rational-activist culture contained within the Civic Culture, but as with those other elements mentioned earlier, these are subsumed within and subordinate to the other domi-nant participant values that define the Civic Culture.

The dominant profile of a citizen in the Civic Culture is that of some-body who is aware of and informed about the status of citizens within democracies, senses the obligation to participate in the process, feels competent to do so and to do so effectively. Such a citizen would affec-tively associate with the democratic regime, usually through a sense of pride and with expectations that the political system will deliver for the public good.

Social cohesion and social capital

This self-confident citizen is bound by multiple social ties: firstly, to primary social groups – those of family, friends, neighbours and the

DOI: 10.1057/9781137496195.0007

workplace; secondly, to formal social groups – mostly interest groups such as churches, labour unions, sport and cultural associations; thirdly, to informal social groups – comprising gregarious individuals with shared interests who coalesce and pursue these interests within the public space through collective effort. As the shared issues fade or are dealt with, these groupings also tend to disperse. These formal and informal formations, taken together, constitute *civil society*, where individuals tend to show high levels of generalised trust in one another instead of suspicion and antagonism. In these formations, members tend to believe that others with similar views will also be inclined to join their cause, rather than act on their own, and they generally uphold the norms of civility in their conduct with one another.[8]

Importantly, the survey data about the Civic Culture of the 1950s, especially in the United Kingdom and United States, show that civil society is composed of a multitude of such associations, with crosscutting membership and moderate partisanship. This prevents the polarisation of society into fixed, opposing and eventually hostile camps. Such polarisation is further prevented by the belief within the Civic Culture that primary groups such as the family are seen to be outside the political domain and not subject to partisan divisions. This form of social cohesion, described as social capital, consists of networks of people who trust and tolerate one another and who act on the basis of norms of reciprocity and consider fellow citizens as social equals. Such social ties serve as an asset to its members, who use it to help one another along in life in a myriad of ways. Furthermore, because these ties are informal and thus invisible, outsiders tend to be mystified, if not infuriated, by the benefits of such social capital to insiders.

Two dimensions of social capital are relevant to this study. Bonding social capital strengthens exclusive categories of networks, such as groups based on ascribed rather than acquired membership criteria, which results in stronger bonds of reciprocity and mutual obligation. By contrast, bridging social capital extends networks across hitherto exclusive social divisions, establishing wider, more inclusive identities and affiliations.[9]

The norm of social equality is of vital importance within the values of social capital and the Civic Culture, as it is key to the discouragement of dispositions of prejudice – another source of social polarisation. The acclaimed social contact hypothesis of Gordon Allport stipulates the conditions essential to this outcome: that all groups in the contact situation accept one another as being of equal status, that they are involved in inter-group co-operation towards common goals and that these actions are approved by authorities, or custom, or by laws.[10]

This hypothesis is present within the Civic Culture as a belief, a firm conviction that good fences do not make for good neighbours, but rather that social engagement makes for a thriving civil society.[11]

The Civic Culture outlined earlier does not accurately reflect the idealised rational-activist model of the democratic citizen. This rational citizen is modelled as an individual who is intensely well-informed about politics, who engages with full commitment and energy into democratic politics at a sustained high level of commitment and who wields influence in public decision-making. In this ideal, the citizen is also a rational, calculating individual, aware of his/her preferences, who is able to rank them in order of importance and to consider the pursuit of each on the basis of dispassionate cost-benefit computations.

Elements of such an orientation are found within the Civic Culture, but these are tempered, modified and muted by a number of other elements of a parochial and subject culture within the Civic Culture. Some of these have been identified in the outline earlier and include the belief that primary group affiliations such as the family are deemed to be beyond the political domain. Likewise, the belief in the obligation to participate in politics is emptied of much aggression by the emotional patriotic orientation towards the political system, pride in the system and an overarching national identity that is also positively evaluated. Also, political objectives are in constant competition with other non-political goals, which are pursued in other personal and social domains.

Almond and Verba concluded their study with the claim that this mix of values is indeed congruent with the political structures of democratic regimes, especially those of the United Kingdom and United States, but they also acknowledged the need to trade off the requirements of citizen effectiveness with system capacity. They recognised that an intensely focussed and super-motivated citizenry may debilitate the system and inhibit effective rule by elected elites. The democratic citizen has to contribute to both aspects of democracy, even if they may contradict one another: '[H]e (she) must be active, yet passive; involved, yet not too involved; influential, yet differential'.[12]

Political cohesion at national level

The final ingredient of the Civic Culture that contributes to social cohesion is that of a sense of community, a 'supra-party solidarity' – a shared

DOI: 10.1057/9781137496195.0007

political identity. This identity arises from the positive affect that is generally accorded by citizens in the Civic Culture to the overall political system. The usual public expression of this shared identity and solidarity is either in patriotism and/or in nationalism. These attitudes, especially as found in the United States and even more so in the United Kingdom at that time, tended to emerge from transgenerational political socialisation, both formal and informal in nature. Almond and Verba also speculated, quite presciently, that new nations without the decades of such socialisation at their disposal would have to 'create' this component of Civic Culture from a symbolic event of overarching, unifying importance, or do so with a symbolic, charismatic leader to serve as a pivot for unity at the symbolic level for such societies.[13] By describing the process in this way, Almond and Verba allow for a process of political socialisation where this inclusive sense of community is a disposition that can be deliberately socially constructed to selectively contain certain features over others, as inclusive and symbolic components.[14]

One thread in this process of shaping the social base of democracy is the role of innovation in communications technology. As presented earlier, an inclusive national identity can emerge in the Civic Culture of mature democracies through a process of both formal and informal political socialisation that proceeds from one generation to the next. Or, if context and circumstance require the more speedy establishment of a cohesive citizenry, a deliberate use of symbols, symbolic events and leaders can be made to 'create' such a collective identity. For Benedict Anderson, the social construction of such a community in the form of a nation is that of the establishment of an *imagined community*.[15]

In this view, the nation is imagined as an inherently sovereign and limited social entity. It is imagined in the sense that nations, even very small ones, consist of thousands of members, the vast majority of whom will never meet one another, but each one, in their mind's eye, is aware of the others and has a sense of him/herself in sharing this particular identity. The nation is sovereign – it is neither being ruled by foreigners, and is limited with defined, albeit malleable, boundaries with other nations, similarly defined. It is, importantly, a *community*, understood as membership with 'deep horizontal comradeship'.[16]

Anderson makes the deliberate point of disowning the interpretation of the imagined nation as a contrived, manufactured social construction, and therefore as not authentic, and as a fabricated and false social entity which, at best, can be taken as a facsimile of the real thing, whatever that

DOI: 10.1057/9781137496195.0007

may be. He insists that beyond primordial kinship, in which groups in small villages lived in daily face-to-face contact situations, all communities are imagined, and all are cultural artefacts, differing only in being constructed in particular ways. For Anderson the emergence of the nation as an imagined community is tightly bound to the technological revolution of the invention of the printing press in Europe in 1454. Up to that time, the pre-eminent imagined communities in Europe were religious, and in continental Europe it was Christian Roman Catholic. This community was bound by the sacred text of the Bible, as written in Latin, and as understood by the religious hierarchy extending from the Vatican. They held an almost hegemonic sway over the average European imagination, being in full control of the primary sources from which imaginary images originate – language in the form of written text.

Gutenberg's new printing presses rapidly broke down this hegemony. By 1500 the incunabula, as an artefact of the earlier period of moveable type, was becoming a thing of the past as more than 20 million books had already been printed in Europe. By 1600 this number was approximately 200 million. The immediate impact of this dramatically new communications network was to contribute to the success of the Protestant Reformation, fast-forwarding the ideas of Martin Luther which he had posted on the door of the Wittenberg Chapel in 1517. His printed works amounted to one-third of all books sold in Germany from 1518 to 1525. Martin Luther became, according to Anderson, the first best-selling author of this new technological age.[17] Notably, the printing press not only facilitated the spread of the ideas of the Reformation, but did so in the German language. This not only broke the monopoly of Latin as a communication medium to gaining transcendent meaning, but also opened the door for other vernacular languages to gain printed status.

Printed texts in these languages, in Anderson's view, also shaped languages in such a way that they became the key to the formation of national identities. Firstly, these new texts became 'unified fields of exchange and communication', whereby speakers of many varieties of a single language could transcend the peculiarities of their particular dialects and find common ground in a shared communication medium in print on paper. This not only broke down barriers within these linguistic communities, but also set up borders with other communities. Secondly, printing contributed, in turn, to the 'fixity' of these languages themselves, that is, in the consolidation and extension of this common ground of linguistic expression, which would eventually lead to the standardisation

DOI: 10.1057/9781137496195.0007

of such languages. Thirdly, newly ranked tiers of languages emerged. Those that gained expression in print became 'languages-of-power' with superior reach to audiences over those languages that only existed as oral expressions. Furthermore, with time, the 'standard' versions of each language gained ascendancy over the other versions as official or state-sanctioned versions.

With print languages thus standardised, and with ever growing rates of literacy allowing for mass consumption of print media, firstly as books, then later and more significantly as newspapers, the daily reading of these materials became what Anderson calls a 'mass ceremony' during which the nation as an imagined community takes form. This occurred through both a private cognitive process and a projected social cognition. As Anderson explained:

> This mass ceremony is performed in silent privacy, in the lair of the skull. Yet each communicant is well aware that the ceremony he performs is being replicated simultaneously by thousands (or millions) of others, of whose existence he is confident, yet of whose identity he has not the slightest notion. Furthermore, this ceremony is incessantly repeated at daily or half-daily intervals throughout the calendar. What more vivid figure for the secular, historically clocked, imagined community can be envisioned? At the same time, the newspaper reader, observing exact replicas of his own paper being consumed by his subway, barbershop, or residential neighbours, is continually reassured that the imagined world is visibly rooted in everyday life.[18]

This print technology contributed much to the formation of national identities in the nineteenth and twentieth centuries, not only in Europe, but eventually globally, in part, as Anderson argued, because the process of forming such imagined communities very quickly assumed a modular character, whereby the details and specific attributes of any particular national identity could be inserted into the substance of the standardised information that was conveyed through the newspaper, radio, pamphlet, poster or book.

This cohesive well-knit citizenry enter democratic politics through efficient institutions for demand generation. The key processes of presenting interests and preferences to policymakers are through that of interest articulation (mostly through organised interest groups) and interest aggregation (mostly political parties), which provide the institutional conveyor belt for taking citizens into electoral politics and from there into representative assemblies where public policy is made. Making decisions about public policy, *inter alia*, on the basis of demands made by

DOI: 10.1057/9781137496195.0007

citizens, is the first crucial step in achieving system capacity. Effective implementation of such policy decisions, when all the while maintaining the constitutional rules that define the regime and its policy-making processes, is the second crucial step, one that delivers legitimacy to the democratic process, which, in turn, is expressed in further public support for the regime. According to Almond and Verba, effective system capacity generated and maintained in this way contributes to maintaining the belief at the very core of the Civic Culture, namely, the myth of citizen competence by providing a partial empirical base for this belief.[19]

These conditions for democracy acquired additional theoretical and political significance when they were contrasted with those of mass societies (also as understood in the mid-twentieth century), which presented the conditions for mobilising people into totalitarian regimes. Mass societies are defined by the very absence of the type of social cohesion on which the Civic Culture rests.

Mass society

The emergence of fascist and communist one-party regimes after the First World War in Europe presented a direct threat to democratic states in the 1930s. From then on through to the end of the Cold War it was imperative for democratic theorists to be able to specify the social origins of totalitarian states and to be able to differentiate them from those of democracies. One of the crucial structural features that drew their attention was the strata of voluntary organisations between the family and the state, now usually described as 'civil society'.

As described earlier, the Civic Culture identifies this layer of social formations (mostly in the form of formal and informal socio-economic interest groups and cultural organisations such as organised religious affiliations) as crucial to the limitation of elite influence on citizens and in constraining the range and intensity of civic action in the public domain. Civil society, therefore, insulated the individual and his/her primary group and state elites from one another. Furthermore, crosscutting membership between the different group affiliations of individuals inhibits social polarisation and, in this way, knits civil society into a cohesive social entity.

The social base of totalitarian regimes represents the polar opposite of the Civic Culture, as described in the works of Hanna Arendt and William Kornhauser.[20] The definitive social condition conducive to the

DOI: 10.1057/9781137496195.0007

formation of such regimes is that of 'mass society', from which mass movements can emerge, and which are susceptible to capture by totalitarian elites. The decline, decay and eventual demise of civil society leads to the formation of an atomised society – the core structural feature of what Kornhauser calls mass society. Individuals, on their own or within their primary group, the family, are neither socially engaged with others nor do they act collectively to achieve shared objectives. There is a sense of the loss of community and the social isolation of individuals. In short, in mass society, most people experience one another as distant strangers, not to be trusted. Social capital, therefore, cannot be re-established in these new urban, industrial settlements. In the absence of this intermediate layer of interest groups, individuals have to deal with the state directly when collective goods are to be pursued, or not at all. The crucial function of social insulation, which civil society provides, is absent: individuals are available and vulnerable to be directly mobilised by elites into mass movements: and elites are, likewise, available and vulnerable to direct pressure from such mass mobilisation – usually in the form of populist movements.

This lack of opportunities for social engagement, according to Kornhauser, impacts adversely on the individual's self-esteem and sense of social worth. The result is self-estrangement, where those who feel alienated from the social order also tend to feel alienated from themselves. Coupled with this sense of alienation there is a sense of powerlessness and a sense that they are unable to act in the public domain as self-contained individuals which leads to generalised anxiety.[21] Not only is there a loss of sense of community, but also a loss of the sense of self, and for such an atomised individual, both personal and social identity then has to be found from external sources.

This condition of atomisation arises from massive and fundamental social dislocation of entire societies. Kornhauser finds this in the conditions of social turmoil created by the processes of industrial capitalist modernisation, all of which were present in continental Europe during the first half of the twentieth century. This entails rapid and comprehensive industrial modernisation with the attendant 'creative destruction' of premodern social structures. It is also present in the instability of financial capitalism where spectacular growth in affluence can be rapidly followed by economic depression, mass unemployment and abject poverty, as occurred with the Great Crash of 1929 and with the global economic depression that lasted until 1934. Most of all it is found

DOI: 10.1057/9781137496195.0007

in war, modern total war, with mass casualties on the front lines, as in the First World War, still known as the Great War. Even more devastating was the effect of the total mobilisation and industrial warfare of the Second World War, with the uprooting of whole societies, the genocide of selected ethnic minorities and the killing of the entire civilian populations of cities such as Dresden, Hiroshima and Nagasaki.

One conceivable outcome of such atomisation is that totalitarian elites, who offer personal identity in ideology, social organisation in the party and abstract objectives in the promised revolutionary future, succeed in mobilising such individuals into mass movements, which then, in turn, are captured by elites who provide a pseudo-community within a totalitarian regime. This is a pseudo-community in the sense that political symbols of national identity are contrived (as are all other such cultural artefacts) as a focus of collective identity and dispersed with the very technology that facilitated the emergence of other imagined communities but as imagined by totalitarian elites only. The crucial difference between such democratic and totalitarian entities is that with the latter, the mass media are fully controlled and censored by state elites and filled with ideologically prescribed content only, making for the comprehensive imposition of collective identities. This was done, as the emerging record of events during the Chinese Communist Revolution show, through propaganda methods that deliberately aimed to inflict self-estrangement and self-alienation in the extreme.[22]

Furthermore, the social institutions of community remain absent and are inhibited from emerging through institutionalised terror by the state over civilians. Friends are encouraged to spy on friends, in order to reveal any presence of counter-revolutionaries and 'enemies of the people' within their own ranks, thus thwarting the emergence of social capital. Even primary groups are penetrated with this directive by the totalitarian state. This process is imposed from above onto families, the core primary group, by setting up parents against children, children against parents, spouse against spouse and brothers and sisters against one another. This is utterly destructive to engendering interpersonal trust and tolerance, the basis of social cohesion and sense of community – thus maintaining the atomised character of a mass society. Civilian engagement with the state in pursuing collective goods remains through the omnipresent and omnipotent *Party*, and/or through social organisations that are formally sanctioned by the leadership.

DOI: 10.1057/9781137496195.0007

With this depiction of the social base of totalitarian states, the case for its direct opposite was thoroughly entrenched. This contrast was a society characterised by a pluralist social organisation, where individuals are: enmeshed with one another in the social ties that make up shared social capital; imbued with the norms of reciprocity; as well as the liberal values of tolerance, interpersonal and generalised trust, and equality as the appropriate social base for democracy.[23] This became a standard reference point in the conceptual and empirical study of democratic political culture and of the social base required for democratic stability,[24] until it was fundamentally challenged twice towards the latter part of the twentieth century.

The first challenge – generally known as the Third Wave of democratisation – was in the form of a set of new democracies that transitioned from previous totalitarian and authoritarian regimes, starting in the mid-1970s. The second challenge emerged from within the stable, established and consolidated democracies such as the United States and those of Western Europe at about the same time. However, this was driven by changes at the core of the capitalist system, with ramifications for the socio-economic security of citizens, and by changes in technology, especially that of television. The forces that shaped the social base within which the TV generation of the 1970s, 1980s and 1990s found themselves presented a new challenge to the maintenance of the Civic Culture in subtle, yet profound ways.

The third wave

This wave of democratisation swept through societies at the edge of the stable democratic core countries. The military coup d'etat in Portugal in April 1974 signalled the start of the so-called Third Wave of democratisation. This followed on a series of previous waves of democratisation, interspersed by reverse waves, sometimes with a slight overlap. Huntington (1991) identified the First Wave as stretching from 1828 to 1926, followed by a reverse wave from 1922 to 1942. The Second Wave lasted from 1943 to 1962 and consisted of democracies that emerged from territories occupied by Italy, Japan and Germany during the Second World War and those that emerged from the process of decolonisation of the European Empires. The second reverse wave stretched from 1958 to 1975.[25] The Third Wave was seen as being

DOI: 10.1057/9781137496195.0007

distinct in many ways, not least of all because its start was considered both implausible and unwitting. It was implausible because in Portugal the military overthrew the Caetano dictatorship, as opposed to the usual target of the military, which is to overthrow democratic regimes. It was unwitting in the sense that the instigators of the coup did not really have in mind the establishment of a democracy in its place.[26] The events in Portugal were rapidly followed by similar ones in Greece and Spain in the next year. This wave then spread to other continents and received additional impetus when communism collapsed as a globally linked political and ideological bloc in 1989, and the Soviet empire was dismantled. After the collapse and disintegration of the USSR, also drawn in were the rump state of Russia as well as its former satellite states in Eastern Europe such as Yugoslavia and Czechoslovakia, and a host of the former Soviet republics such as the Central Asian Islamic republics, and Ukraine, Belarus and the three Baltic states of Latvia, Lithuania and Estonia.

This produced the highpoint of optimism about the prospects for liberal democracy as the unchallenged prescription for progress and stability, eloquently expressed by Francis Fukuyama in a widely acclaimed essay.[27] Yet here, democratic regimes were being established on an often very inauspicious social base. Some of these societies were embroiled in longstanding civil conflicts, if not civil wars. The adversaries, more often than not, configured themselves into ethnically defined incipient whole societies within the boundaries of the state. Social capital was directed inwards into bonding these discrete social units but with bridging social capital conspicuous by its absence. The social base of these societies tended to be fragmented, with social cleavages being mutually reinforcing rather than crosscutting, with the cleavage between rich and poor, black and white, settler and indigene, Catholic and Protestant, Muslim and Christian invariably separating the same people into antagonistic groups over and over again. Even where such clear-cut polarisation was not evident, crosscutting affiliations provided little overall social cohesion as these affiliations were trumped by the more salient identity of ethnicity.[28] The crucial question about this Third Wave of democratisation was whether these new democratic regimes would be able to hold the centre long enough in the absence of the necessary preconditions for success, so as to create the required conditions in this fractured social base to sustain themselves. Or would this wave be followed by a backwash that would undo this democratic surge?

DOI: 10.1057/9781137496195.0007

A variety of conceptual frameworks were developed with which to make sense of these democratising events. One was to consider these events as part and parcel of peace processes, and that the standardised procedures, strategies and tactics of bargaining and negotiation (as established in the field of diplomacy and industrial relations) would identify the key variables that shape the process.[29] A second one was to focus less on process, but to look at the negotiated outcomes, in the form of constitutions, as key to understanding the Third Wave.[30] The third approach, one most relevant to this study, is the school of thought that came to be known as the transition paradigm.[31] This perspective finds the explanatory variables in the power relations between the old outgoing elites and the new incoming elites. Most importantly, they found, on the basis of the then examples from Southern Europe and South America, that democratic theory could discard the core propositions that successful democracies tend to emerge from particular socio-economic conditions (what we call here the social base) and that the stern warning by Huntington that 'there are no shortcuts to political salvation'[32] could be dispensed with. In one presentation of this paradigm, Schmitter completely inverted these two propositions, and reversed the causal sequence between preconditions and outcomes. He argued (writing in 1994) that the empirical cases of transition had, by then, shown that democratic transitions could and did occur without preconditions such as: (i) a relatively high level of economic development; (ii) a significant narrowing of the income gap between top and bottom earners; (iii) the presence of a strong middle class (which he refers to as a 'national bourgeoisie'); and (iv) a Civic Culture. These conditions, he argued, may well become significant in the longer term for democratic stability, but 'they are likely to be produced by its regular functioning' and, in any case, are not necessary for democratic transition or consolidation.[33]

Events on the ground did not bear out this optimism. Towards the close of the century, Larry Diamond raised the question of whether the Third Wave had run its course and if it was about to move into a reverse wave.[34] He noted that some of the pivotal success stories, such as Brazil, Turkey, Nigeria and especially Russia, were showing indications of 'increasing shallowness'. By this he meant that such cases were moving away from being liberal democracies[35] with extensive civil and political rights, to instances of becoming electoral democracies or pseudo-democracies. Both regime categories were examples of 'illiberal' democracies and could also be described as hybrid regimes, where some of the formal characteristics of democratic politics, such as elections, are present, but where authentic contestation for power is absent, and a dominant party sets the uneven playing field.[36] Research has confirmed that the apparent global consensus on the preference for democracy should be considered at best, in some cases, as little more than paying lip service to this regime type.[37]

By 2002, the validity of the transition paradigm was seriously questioned. In reviewing the Third Wave, Thomas Carothers found less than 20 fully successful democratic transitions, with about 80 cases which, as he described, have moved into a political 'gray zone'.[38] Two regime types can be identified in this grey zone: that of dominant party regimes and another characterised by feckless pluralism. In both regime types, civil society experiences a torrid time. In dominant party regimes, the ruling party tries to merge party and state and uses state power to harass, intimidate and suppress opposition, allowing only voting as an avenue of participation. In regimes with feckless pluralism, such as Nicaragua, Ecuador, Nepal, Ukraine, Madagascar and Guinea-Bissau (at the time of his writing), where seemingly corrupt elites from one party tend to be replaced by much of the same from rival parties, the citizenry end up being deeply disaffected with what is held up as new democracy, and they tend to shy away from active civic and political engagement.

At the time of his writing Carothers still placed Russia (along with South Africa) at the edge of the grey zone. By 2007, however, after a deeply flawed election, Russia moved into that zone and has subsequently been classified as 'not free' by Freedom House.[39] Carothers also noted that some of the more durable transitions have been in Taiwan, Mexico and South Korea, where no shortcuts were taken, and multi-party democracy has been achieved against long-ruling dominant parties through incremental gains by opposition parties over decades.[40] He concluded that the argument about necessary preconditions for successful democratic transitions remain valid. Without a particular social base, the prospects for democratic success remain dim.

Television and the decline of social capital

The research for Almond and Verba's *The Civic Culture* was conducted in Italy, Great Britain, West Germany and Mexico in 1959 and in the United States in 1960. The book was first published in 1963. In November of that

DOI: 10.1057/9781137496195.0007

very year, President John F. Kennedy was assassinated. This is generally taken as the signal event for the start of the 1960s, an era of political, cultural and ideological turmoil in many democracies, but especially so in the United States. This unprecedented process of cultural combustion set in motion a political process which came to challenge the continued validity of this empirical description of stable, effective and legitimate democracy, especially in the United States. What was valid in 1959 and 1960 was, for a large part, invalidated within a generation. The 1960s generated challenges to the political culture that, up to then, had buttressed the more or less standardised procedures for achieving both citizen effectiveness and system capacity in democracies – challenges that persist in the contemporary era. The impact of the next innovation in mass communication on democratic political culture – colour television – will be considered next.

On the basis of research spanning the post–Second World War era in the United States, Robert Putnam found that a marked rise in social capital up to the mid-1960s was followed by an equally significant decline through to the end of the century.[41] His data show a decline in many, if not most, forms of civic engagement, ranging from a decline in church attendance, the visiting of neighbours and friends and a decline in contributions to philanthropic causes. Most marked was the fall in formal group membership, the backbone of civil society, and the institutional core of the Civic Culture. In addition, the core value of social trust also declined steeply.

A number of factors were found to account for this trend. Firstly, the changing character of American capitalism, with the rise of two-career families and the attendant pressure on the free time available for additional community-based voluntarism was identified, but only about 10 per cent of the decline in social capital was attributable to this factor. Secondly, the process of sub-urbanisation, with the attendant sprawl and increasing distance between home and workplace, also factored in. More time was being spent on commuting, making less time available for voluntary civic action, but again, only 10 per cent of the decline was linked to this factor. Thirdly, about 25 per cent of the decline was attributed to the rise of electronic entertainment, mostly through colour television. Television has privatised entertainment, keeping individuals and families at home, thus increasing their social isolation. The fourth and most significant factor, according to Putnam, was that of generational change. The most engaged generation civically were those born

DOI: 10.1057/9781137496195.0007

and raised during the first third of the twentieth century, whom Putnam calls 'the long civic generation' (those born more or less between 1910 and 1940), as they were more engaged and more trusting than every other subsequent generation (with his data covering the years up to about 1969). Consequently, half of the decline in social capital is attributed to this generational change. The last two factors are to some extent intertwined, so Putnam adds another 10–15 per cent to the joint effect of TV and generational change, making the 'TV-generation' a distinct explanatory factor (the remaining 20 per cent of the decline in social capital he left unaccounted for).[42]

Putnam's findings were challenged on various grounds, such as the analysis produced by Norris (1996), who argued that the facts show that it is TV content, rather than hours spent before the TV that could be the crucial factor in accounting for its impact on American public life.[43] The more comprehensive and thoughtful response was from Bennett,[44] who produced less of a rebuttal, and instead, a new and wider framework for interpreting Putnam's data.

Bennett took note of the decline in social engagement in the United States reported by Putnam, but interpreted this as not so much a decline in social engagement but as a shift from established formally institutionalised channels of civic participation towards new forms of political action, driven by newly defined interests. The decline in conventional channels of engagement such as church activities and lower levels of confidence in national political institutions had, according to Bennett, been matched by a rise of so-called lifestyle groups, and a shift towards individualised rather than collectively defined interests. For Bennett this was the advent of 'politics by other means', and this shift coincided with the time when colour TV reached saturation point within the American consumer market.

The driving force in this re-alignment of interests, and of interest-driven political engagement, is, according to Bennett, to be found in what he calls the 'new economy'. At the core of this economy, he argues, is a labour force that is facing increasing social dislocation, rising monetary and job-tenure insecurity and increasing uncertainty about their economic prospects, which has led to a generalised sense of anxiety. The structural changes that emerged from the early 1970s in the American economy and which instigated this set of dispositions are to be found in: (i) the shift from manufacturing to service economic activity; (ii) a widening of income differentials between the upper 20 per cent

DOI: 10.1057/9781137496195.0007

and the bottom 10 per cent of wage earners; (iii) increasing work hours; (iv) the large-scale entry of women into the labour market; (v) the rise of two-parent working families; and (vi) the rise in temporary and contract employment over tenured positions.[45]

Opinion surveys of the late 1980s and 1990s found high levels of value confusion among respondents. One survey (reported in 1998) found that 80 per cent of men and women felt that the new conditions of work, family and social life had made it more difficult to raise children, and 70 per cent of them also felt these conditions also had made it harder for marriages to succeed. Rising work stress was also measured as a result of longer working hours (just to maintain living standards) and rising personal and household debt. These conditions had led to problems that were increasingly defined as personal, rather than collective public issues, about which a distant federal government would have little insight, let alone be able to remedy. The overall impact of the conditions of personal and social upheaval that originated in job losses, underemployment, career changes, changing family roles, less personal leisure time and less time for personal and family relationships has been on the fragmentation of civil society, and the personalisation of political concerns. The combined effect of such individualisation, globalisation and secularisation would lead to the formation of new, post-materialist values.[46] This, according to Bennett (writing in 1998), was leading to a fundamental shift '[b]ecause personal identity is replacing collective identity as the basis for contemporary political engagement, the character of politics itself is changing'. In addition, he noted, quite presciently for the time which was just before the era of digital social media, that '[n]owhere has this change been more pronounced than in the development and uses of sophisticated communication technologies to shape political perceptions and affiliations'.[47] These media, he predicted, were set to take over the core functions of interest aggregation thus far executed by political parties and elections.

In looking ahead from his vantage point of 1998, Bennett was not optimistic about the psychological impact of this new economy with the new communication technology. Both were, in tandem, creating an isolating effect that adversely impacted on the individual psyche. He warned that the emotional well-being of individuals may be eroded by their difficulty in establishing a sense of shared identity that could reach across different social and political settings. Furthermore, he continued, there is the prospect of individuals finding it more and more difficult to

DOI: 10.1057/9781137496195.0007

identify with the 'collective symbols of the imagined communities that we call nations'.[48]

The problem, as he saw it, was very similar to the danger found by Kornhauser in the collective entity of the mass society; a loss of personal identity leaves a psychological vacuum that the vulnerable individual needs to fill. For Kornhauser that danger was that the atomised individual would succumb to the pseudo-community offered by totalitarian elites. Instead, Bennett senses that Americans who experience such a loss of secure identities are moving in a different direction: they consume more and more prescription tranquillisers and other such chemical substances, and in that way slide into deeper social isolation. He concluded with the question of whether the new media would be able to construct new 'supportive virtual subcultures' that could actually supply 'the emotional bases for individual identity, acceptance, and empathy – factors that also contribute to the quality and health of a polity'. This question was framed by him as: 'How can communication technologies be adapted to the deliberation, interest formation, and decision-making requirements of societies that may be better positioned to experiment with direct democracy than any other in history?'[49] This is very close to the question we posed at the start of this chapter: Can digital media, including social media, contribute to creating new and durable imagined communities favourable to the reconstruction of the social base of these democracies?

Conclusion

One of the effects of the third reverse wave was to raise doubts about the global viability of liberal democracy as a model for governing societies. This unease is expressed in the recognition that it is a model that sets stringent conditions for its effective functioning. These conditions are found in, *inter alia*, (i) the values and norms that shape the civic political culture and human rights doctrine; (ii) the socio-economic conditions of modernity (expressed in many ways, but mostly through material affluence); (iii) relative socio-economic equality; and (iv) the presence of the United States as a benign global hegemony in protecting democracies against the totalitarian threats of twentieth-century fascism and communism. In all these factors the role of path dependence and contingency can be seen, which makes the success of democracy itself a unique historical and cultural phenomenon, not easily replicated everywhere.[50]

DOI: 10.1057/9781137496195.0007

Likewise, the continuously evolving economic system of capitalism, with the inherent creative 'destruction' of ever new technologies has, towards the close of the twentieth century, put the historic correlation between capitalism and democracy under increasing strain and continuously renews the question of the viability of democratic institutions in this new technological age. This process, which is still under way, is disrupting the social base of even the most well-established democracies in ways that have yet to be fully experienced and therefore, yet to be fully understood. What is important for democrats is to retain awareness of what the levels of support for democracy are, and how it is changing throughout this process, in order to grasp the dynamics of the new social base in which democracy is embedded, and also to assess the viability of standard democratic procedures on a continual basis. In the next chapter we consider both established and new ways of measuring support for democracy.

Notes

1   A. Gat (2006) *War in Human Civilization* (Oxford: Oxford University Press), pp. 445, 449.

2   S.E. Finer (1997) *The History of Government from the Earliest Times. Vol. II: The Intermediate Ages* (New York: Oxford University Press), chapter 8, esp. pp. 1024–1051.

3   R.A. Dahl and E.R. Tufte (1973) *Size and Democracy* (Stanford, CA: Stanford University Press), p. 20.

4   Dahl and Tufte, *Size and Democracy*, p. 5.

5   S.E. Finer (1997) *The History of Government from the Earliest Times, Vol. I: Ancient Monarchies and Empires* (Oxford: Oxford University Press), p. 341.

6   Dahl and Tufte, *Size and Democracy*, pp. 20–23.

7   G.A. Almond and S. Verba (1963/1965) *The Civic Culture. Political Attitudes and Democracy in Five Nations* (Boston: Little, Brown and Company).

8   E. Shils (1991) 'The Virtue of Civil Society', *Government and Opposition*, 26, Winter, 3–20.

9   For an overview of the concept of social capital, its sources and its consequences, see D. Stolle (2007) 'Social Capital', in R. Dalton and H.-D. Klingeman (eds), *The Oxford Handbook of Political Behavior* (New York: Oxford University Press), pp. 655–674.

10   G. Allport (1954) *The Nature of Prejudice* (Cambridge, MA: Addison-Wesley), p. 281. Studies that confirm this hypothesis are summarised in T.F. Pettigrew and L.R. Tropp (2006) 'A Meta-analytic Test of Intergroup Contact Theory',

DOI: 10.1057/9781137496195.0007

Journal of Personality and Social Psychology, 90(5), 751–783. An elaboration of this theory is found in T.F. Pettigrew (2006) 'Intergroup Contact Theory', *Annual Review of Psychology*, 49, 65–85.

11　See also J. Duckitt (2003) 'Prejudice and Intergroup Hostility', in D.O. Sears, L. Huddy and R. Jervis (eds), *Oxford Handbook of Political Psychology* (New York: Oxford University Press), pp. 559–600.

12　Almond and Verba, *The Civic Culture*, p. 343, 344.

13　Almond and Verba, *The Civic Culture*, p. 372.

14　Where this process of inclusive national identity formation failed, it invariably occurred in territories with multi-cultural populations, where these sub-cultural entities came to be the units of collective identity formation, to the point where each of these entities came to see (imagine) themselves as *incipient whole societies*, and where they raised public demands accordingly. In societies deeply divided in this way, democratic stability, even democracy of any quality, has been extremely difficult to maintain, and its concomitant features of a civil society that is embedded in a civic culture has been conspicuous by its absence. Majority domination, civil war, authoritarian repression and the threat of secession have been recurring features of these political entities for much of the nineteenth and twentieth centuries. Post-communist Yugoslavia as well as Nigeria, Northern Ireland, South Africa, Rwanda, Burundi, Somalia and Lebanon are some of the regimes which experienced almost perennial political upheaval for many decades. Finding appropriate constitutional rules for the maintenance of democracy in these types of societies with the absence of civic cultures became one of the leading challenges for democratic theory in the latter half of the twentieth century. See D.L. Horowitz (1985) *Ethnic Groups in Conflict* (Berkeley: University of California Press).

15　B. Anderson (2006) *Imagined Communities. Reflections on the Origin and Spread of Nationalism*, revised edn (London: Verso).

16　Anderson, *Imagined Communities*, pp. 6, 7.

17　Anderson, *Imagined Communities*, p. 39.

18　Anderson, *Imagined Communities*, p. 35. Used with permission from Verso Press.

19　Anderson, *Imagined Communities*, p. 354.

20　H. Arendt (1951) *The Origins of Totalitarianism* (New York: Harcourt, Brace and Company); W. Kornhauser (1960) *The Politics of Mass Society* (London: Routledge and Kegan Paul). For a partially dissenting view, see J.J. Linz (2000) *Totalitarian and Authoritarian Regimes* (Boulder, CO: Lynne Rienner Press).

21　Kornhauser, *The Politics of Mass Society*, p. 108, 109.

22　F. Dikötter (2013) *The Tragedy of Liberation. A History of the Chinese Revolution, 1945–57* (London: Bloomsbury).

DOI: 10.1057/9781137496195.0007

23 D. Fuchs (2007) 'The Political Culture Paradigm', in Dalton and Klingeman (eds), *The Oxford Handbook of Political Behavior*, pp. 161–184; and F. Sabetti (2007) 'Democracy and Civic Culture', in C. Boix and S.C. Stokes (eds), *The Oxford Handbook of Comparative Politics* (New York: Oxford University Press), pp. 340–362. For a summary of the debate on whether political culture is a cause or consequence of political structure and the reasons for the continued salience of culture in the analysis of collective action in contemporary global events, see L. Halman (2007) 'Political Values', in Dalton and Klingeman (eds), *The Oxford Handbook of Political Behavior* (New York: Oxford University Press), pp. 305–322, and also J. Thomassen (2007) 'Democratic Values', in Dalton and Klingeman (eds), *The Oxford Handbook of Political Behavior* (New York: Oxford University Press), pp. 418–434.

24 R.A. Dahl (1971) *Polyarchy. Participation and Opposition* (New Haven, CT: Yale University Press); G.A. Almond and G.B. Powell Jr. (1966) *Comparative Politics, a Developmental Approach* (Boston: Little, Brown & Co); S.M. Lipset (1959/1981) *Political Man. The Social Bases of Politics* (Baltimore, MD: Johns Hopkins University Press).

25 S.P. Huntington (1991) *The Third Wave. Democratization in the Late Twentieth Century* (Norman: Oklahoma University Press), pp. 13–26.

26 Huntington, *The Third Wave*, pp. 3, 4.

27 F. Fukuyama (1989) 'The End of History', *The National Interest*, 16, 3–18.

28 A. Rabushka and K.A. Shepsle (1972) *Politics in Plural Societies. A Theory of Democratic Instability* (Columbus, OH: Charles E. Merrill), pp. 55–61.

29 P. Harris and B. Reilly (eds) (1998) *Democracy and Deep-Rooted Conflict: Options for Negotiators* (Stockholm: International Idea); J. Darby and R. Mac Ginty (eds) (2008) *Contemporary Peacemaking. Conflict, Peace Processes and Post-war Reconstruction*, 2nd edn (Basingstoke: Palgrave Macmillan); H. Miall, O. Ramsbotham and T. Woodhouse (2011) *Contemporary Conflict Resolution*, 3rd edn (Cambridge: Polity Press).

30 Some of the leading works are by A. Lijphart (1977) *Democracy in Plural Societies. A Comparative Exploration* (New Haven, CT: Yale University Press); Horowitz, *Ethnic Groups in Conflict*; T.D. Sisk (1995) *Power-Sharing and International Mediation in Ethnic Conflict* (Washington, DC: United States Institute of Peace Press); R. Taylor (ed.) (2009) *Consociational Theory. McGarry and O'Leary and the Northern Ireland Conflict* (London: Routledge).

31 G. O'Donnell, P.C. Schmitter and L. Whitehead (eds) (1986) *Transitions from Authoritarian Rule. Prospects for Democracy* (London: Johns Hopkins University Press).

32 S.P. Huntington (1988) 'One Soul at a Time: Political Science and Political Reform', *American Political Science Review*, 82(1), 9.

DOI: 10.1057/9781137496195.0007

33   P.C. Schmitter (1994) 'The Proto-Science of Consolidology: Can It Improve the Outcome of Contemporary Efforts at Democratization?', *Politikon, South African Journal of Political Studies*, 21(3), 15–27, at 25.

34   L. Diamond (1996) 'Is the Third Wave Over?', *Journal of Democracy*, 7(3), 20–37.

35   F. Zakaria (1997) 'The Rise of Illiberal Democracy', *Foreign Affairs*, November/December, 22–43.

36   L. Diamond (2002) 'Elections without Democracy: Thinking about Hybrid Regimes', *Journal of Democracy*, 13(2), 21–35. Also relevant is S. Levitsky and L. Way (2002) 'The Rise of Competitive Authoritarianism', *Journal of Democracy*, 13(2), 51–65.

37   D.C. Shin (2007) 'Democratization: Perspectives from Global Citizenries', in Dalton and Klingeman (eds), *The Oxford Handbook of Political Behavior* (New York: Oxford University Press), pp. 259–282.

38   T. Carothers (2002) 'The End of the Transition Paradigm', *Journal of Democracy*, 13(1), 5–21.

39   P. Hassner (2008) 'Russia's Transition to Autocracy', *Journal of Democracy*, 19(2), 5–15. Freedom House is a non-profit organization, established in 1941, that rates countries annually in terms of their political freedom. This proceeds along two dimensions, the first being Political Rights and the second Civil Liberties. Each country is graded on a scale of 1–7 for each dimension, with most free counties scoring 1 and least free countries scoring 7 on each scale. Then the combined totals are compared and categorised into three categories: 'Free' (countries with average scores of between 1 and 2.5), 'Partly Free' (for countries with rankings of 3.0–5.0) and 'Not Free' (countries who score between 5.5 and 7). See also J. Moller and S.-E. Skaaning (2013) 'The Third Wave: Inside the Numbers', *Journal of Democracy*, 24(4), 97–109. In this study of the global distribution of regime types with data from 1972 till 2012 the expansion of the grey zone is confirmed.

40   For an analysis of the transition from dominant party regimes to multi-party democracies in Mexico, Taiwan and South Korea, see N. de Jager and P. du Toit (eds) (2013) *Friend or Foe?, Dominant Party Systems in Southern Africa. Insights from the Developing World* (Claremont, CA: University of Claremont Press; and Tokyo: United Nations University Press).

41   R.D. Putnam (2000) *Bowling Alone. The Collapse and Revival of American Community* (New York: Simon & Schuster); R.D. Putnam (1995) 'Turning In, Tuning Out: The Strange Disappearance of Social Capital in America', *PS, Political Science & Politics*, XXVIII(4), 664–683.

42   Putnam, *Bowling Alone*, pp. 283, 284. Subsequent research has confirmed that this may in fact be a peculiarly American phenomenon. See D. Stolle (2007) 'Social Capital', in Dalton and Klingeman (eds), *The Oxford Handbook of Political Behavior* (New York: Oxford University Press), pp. 655–674.

DOI: 10.1057/9781137496195.0007

43   P. Norris (1996) 'Does Television Erode Social Capital? A Reply to Putnam,' *PS Political Science and Politics*, XXIX, 474–479.

44   W.L. Bennett (1998) 'The UnCivic Culture: Communication, Identity, and the Rise of Lifestyle Politics', *PS, Political Science and Politics*, XXXI(4), 741–762.

45   Bennett, 'The UnCivic Culture', 750–753.

46   L. Halman, 'Political Values', in Dalton and Klingeman (eds), *The Oxford Handbook of Political Behavior* (New York: Oxford University Press), pp. 310–316.

47   Bennett, 'The UnCivic Culture', 755.

48   Bennett, 'The UnCivic Culture', 757.

49   Bennett, 'The UnCivic Culture', 758.

50   Gat, *War in Human Civilization*, pp. 557–621.

DOI: 10.1057/9781137496195.0007

3

The Development of Methods for Measuring Expressions on Democracy

Abstract: *Chapter 3 is divided into four broad sections. Firstly, the value of measuring expressions on democracy is briefly examined. Secondly, an examination of traditional methods of measuring expressions on democracy can be found. Thirdly, Twitter is examined as a new form of Habermasian public sphere. Finally, a section on novel emerging methods of measuring public expressions from online sources is found. This section specifically looks at a number of recent studies which have utilised Twitter in order to gauge public expressions. The broad aim of this chapter is to illustrate novel methods – such as the method developed in this book – that might lead to an alternative method of measurement. We do not claim that this method will replace traditional methods of measuring expressions on democracy; but we do believe that it could supplement and enhance the data gathered using traditional methods.*

Keywords: Habermas; public opinion; public sphere; survey research; Twitter

Lutz, Barend and Pierre du Toit. *Defining Democracy in a Digital Age: Political Support on Social Media.* Basingstoke: Palgrave Macmillan, 2014. DOI: 10.1057/9781137496195.0008.

Some believe that, globally, citizens are steadily becoming more critical of politicians, political parties and political policies, that is, of the whole democratic process. These negative sentiments might be indicative of what Van Beek[1] calls 'an erosion in support for democracy'. However, as mentioned in the previous chapter, this potential disrupting of the social base still needs deeper examination. In this chapter, the intrinsic value of understanding public opinions on democracy is examined. In recent times there have been a multitude of academics, government institutions, think tanks and other organisations that focus on exploring public opinion on democracy. An extract of this field will be presented so as to locate the approach for measuring democracy with the methods developed in this book. This will illustrate how one can extend the value of the traditional survey-based research by utilising alternative sources of opinion-rich data, namely, Twitter.

The value of measuring expressions on democracy

With the evolution and the potential recent erosion of democracy in mind, two questions now emerge: what are the current public expressions on democracy, and can one gauge the 'habits of the heart' that are prevalent in contemporary society? Before answering these questions, it is important to note that there is inherent value in measuring expressions on democracy. This intrinsic value highlights the need for a well-functioning society to understand mass attitudes on the subject of democracy.

Traditional studies measuring democracy find value in these measurements beyond exploring global tides of political governance and waves of democracy examined earlier. There is also an inherent value to understanding the functioning of any democratic political system, and also in how the different parts of the system fit together and their role and position in the bigger system. In a democracy, where the *voice of the people*, at least in theory, is supposed to govern, understanding this *voice* is paramount to the continued existence and prosperity of the system. Traditional literature on the value of public opinion to the democratic consolidation and functioning of democracies, examined later, provides one with a good understanding and respect for the value of measuring expressions on democracy. There are a number of studies that examine the value of public opinions to the democratic consolidation and functioning of democracies.

DOI: 10.1057/9781137496195.0008

Within the academic school of political culture, there exists the belief that the functioning and persistence of democracy and democratic institutions is integrally linked with dominant mass tendencies in individual-level attitudes and value orientations.[2] The rationale for the link between opinions of citizens and the functioning of a democracy is based on the idea of a public sphere. This refers to a physical or virtual space where the public can meet to discuss, debate and deliberate on public affairs. The public sphere lies between state and society and is an essential component of socio-political organisation: it provides a form of legitimacy and accountability to a government and a space for citizens to participate in public affairs.[3]

Those who study democracy have noted that the hallmark of a well-functioning consolidated democracy is the unconditional embrace of the citizenry of democracy as 'the only game in town'.[4] The belief in the legitimacy of the democratic system by the citizens of a democracy has become a central tenet of a stable democracy.[5]

With the potential of a crisis – or 'an erosion of democracy', as Van Beek[6] calls it – it is important to understand and analyse the functioning of democracies across the world. With this in mind, after the Third Wave of democratisation, there has been a rise in studies looking specifically at the level of democratic consolidation in new and old democratic regimes. These studies can be broadly divided into two main traditions.

Firstly, there are scholars such as Horowitz,[7] Lijphart[8] and Sisk[9] who have focussed on the institutionalisation and habituation of political practices and institutions. They examine how, through constitutional design, the best procedures and institutions for democratic governance can be attained. This approach, therefore, focusses primarily on the more structural design aspects of a democracy. If the institutional framework of a democracy is healthy, these authors would argue that the democracy would have a better chance to be successfully habituated and finally consolidated.

Secondly, there are researchers from Almond and Verba[10] through to Inglehart[11] and his associates who have examined the practices and values of civil societies, together with the attitudes and values of the citizenry, to gauge the level of democratic quality of a country. The methodology developed in this book broadly falls into this second category as it is argued that the quality of the institutions in a democratic regime is not the only aspect for democratic consolidation. One should also look at the attitudes of the citizens participating in the democratic process to

DOI: 10.1057/9781137496195.0008

understand the level of democratic consolidation. The rationale is that if there are high levels of support for sustained democratic governance within the citizenry, democracy will tend to flourish. The opposite also holds true: if the populace of a democracy does not support the institutions of democracy, or democracy itself, then democracy, in the long term, is doomed to failure. Even if the democratic institutions are of a high standard in such a case, it could lack general support and subsequently fail.

To many scholars this perhaps sounds like an obvious point to make. In fact, Inglehart[12] has stated that the measurement of overt support for democracy in a democratic system has obvious face value, seeing that a lack of support for a political system based on majority support would raise serious questions as to the validity and legitimacy of such a system. He backs up this claim in his 2003 study, 'How Solid Is Mass Support for Democracy: And How Can We Measure It?' In this study, World Values Survey (WVS) data for the period 1981–2000 was used to show that if one examines the long-term stability of democracy, positive attitudes towards democracy are a good indicator of this stability.

A good way to understand further the aforementioned distinction between the two main traditions for studying democratic consolidation is the explanation offered by Rose, Mishler and Haerpfer.[13] They have compared political institutions to the 'hardware' of democratic systems, and the opinion of the citizens on these institutions to the 'software' of the system. Extending this metaphor, they state that just as a computer cannot function without the combination of both hardware and software, a democratic system cannot function without proper institutions and public support for these institutions. Although both factors are clearly important, more focus has been placed in our book on the software, namely, the support for democracy. However, before one gets to our unique measurement methodology, one should explore a number of the traditional approaches and studies that are being used to measure support for democracy today. It should be noted that there is an ongoing debate on finding appropriate measurement methodologies for measuring mass attitudes on democracy and defining democracy, and the research here only serves as an introduction to this debate.[14] By examining these traditional studies of democracy we can begin to note certain patterns that most studies of democracy seem to follow.

DOI: 10.1057/9781137496195.0008

Traditional methods of measuring public expressions on democracy

In 1981 the WVS broke new ground by becoming the largest global research project to explore people's values and beliefs. Today, this expansive study collects data from almost 100 societies (nearly 90% of the world's population), and this data is available freely online.[15] The collection of these surveys shows in great detail how values and beliefs impact the political and social spheres and also how these beliefs change over time. The WVS has also highlighted intergenerational changes taking place in basic values relating to politics, economic life, religion, gender roles and family and sexual norms. In addition, and most relevant to our study's question regarding the measurement of democracy, the WVS survey has aimed to explore the cultural conditions that are needed in a society to support a well- consolidated democracy. Since the third wave of the WVS survey conducted in 1995–1997, the programme has been monitoring public support of democracy and democratic institutions. However, it should be noted that the WVS is only one of the many better-known empirical research programmes monitoring public opinion and its influence on democracy. Some other well-known programmes are: (i) the AfroBarometer; (ii) the European Values Study; (iii) the New Russia Barometer; (iv) and the LatinoBarometer. Each of these programmes has sections in their surveys that aim at gauging individual support for democracy. These individual levels of support can then be tallied to show mass expressions of support for democracy in a specific area.

In this chapter some these aforementioned traditional methods and institutions measuring expressions on democracy will be described, most notably the WVS and their methodology, to show how they sought to find accurate, efficient, timely and representative measurements of democracy. The broad goal is to illustrate how global and localised measurements of democracy take place. Although only some of the questions that are examined in these traditional survey methods about democracy will be presented, this will give a baseline for the creation of an independent method as it will demonstrate the type of information that such a method should attempt to gather. The traditional survey methods are well established and form a solid foundation upon which to attempt their expansion by using new technologies such as Twitter.[16]

The aim of this presentation is to illustrate the actual survey items, whether questions or statements, that are used to measure dispositions

DOI: 10.1057/9781137496195.0008

towards democracy. It is not the objective to discuss or evaluate the various ways in which multiple survey items have been combined in order to create multi-dimensional value constructs which serve as correlates of, or determinants of democracy, as has been done with great sophistication by Inglehart and his associates.[17]

Such an examination can be split into two broad groups, namely: (i) global research projects, looking at values across nation states; and (ii) regional research projects that are more localised. The two research projects that examine attitudes and expressions on democracy on a global level will be presented first.

The world values survey

The WVS identifies itself as '[t]he world's most comprehensive investigation of political and sociocultural change', and it is the most well-known global research project on democracy, which examines the opinions, values and beliefs of citizens. For the purposes of this book, the established 2005–2009 wave was examined. However, it should be noted that the new sixth wave of the survey, from 2010 to 2014, was released in April 2014 at the General Assembly meeting in Doha, Qatar. Both surveys used in these most recent waves contain a number of sub-sections about democracy. In the 2005–2009 (fifth) wave, the most direct question regarding the support for democracy is in section V162, the results of which follow in Table 3.1:

> V162. *How important is it for you to live in a country that is governed democratically? On this scale where 1 means it is not at all important and 10 means absolutely important – what position would you choose?*

TABLE 3.1 *WVS: question V162 – the importance of democracy*

		Total
	Not at all important	1.50%
	2	0.50%
	3	0.70%
	4	1.10%
	5	5.90%
V 162: Importance of democracy	6	4.70%
	7	7.40%
	8	14.10%
	9	14.40%
	Absolutely important	49.60%
	Total	73,986 (100%)

Source: World Values Survey.

DOI: 10.1057/9781137496195.0008

From the results of respondents of the 57 countries in this round, a majority (90.20%) answered between 6 and 10, which can broadly be seen as being in support of democracy. The strong support for democracy is particularly evident when one notes that 49.60 per cent of respondents believed that it is absolutely important for them to live in a country that is governed democratically.[18]

The second question relating to democracy is V151. The results for this question can be found in Table 3.2. It asked respondents about their views on various types of political systems, including democracies. The question read:

> V151. I'm going to describe various types of political systems and ask what you think about each as a way of governing this country. For each one, would you say it is a very good, fairly good, fairly bad or very bad way of governing this country? Having a democratic political system?

The results of Question V151 on opinions of democracy as a political system showed that 91.6 per cent of the respondents believed that having a democratic political system was a fairly or very good way of governing their own countries. What both results from questions V162 and V151 showed was that, globally, people were broadly in support of democracy as a political system and would like to live in a democracy.

Consequently, if one only looks at these questions and the responses during this round of the WVS, it would seem that global support for democracy is healthy; however, it will be interesting to compare these figures from the fifth wave of the survey (2005–2007) to the latest figures released in April 2014. It should also be noted the WVS findings earlier only show a broad support for democratic governance and democracy as a political system and do not necessarily indicate a deep-set support for the institutions of democracy. It falls outside of the scope of this book to examine the various waves of the WVS in more detail, but it should

TABLE 3.2   *WVS: question V151– opinions on a democratic political system*

		Total
V151: Political system: a democratic political system	Very good	51.50%
	Fairly good	40.10%
	Fairly bad	6.30%
	Very bad	2.20%
	Total	73,787 (100%)

Source: World Values Survey.

DOI: 10.1057/9781137496195.0008

be noted that more information on the support for democracy and its institutions can be found in the WVS. The important aspect to note here is the format of questioning that the WVS used to indicate broad global opinions of democracy. Such an approach will also be incorporated in the methodology of this present research.

Voice of the people

A second global survey run by Gallup International Association is known as Voice of the People (VOTP).[19] This annual international survey from 2002 to 2005 examined opinions of respondents from more than 50 countries on various social elements, one of which was opinion on democracy. For the purposes of this study, the two relevant items that this survey presented to respondents about democracy were in the format of statements to which they were asked to respond:

1   In general I am satisfied with democracy. (Agree/Disagree)
2   Democracy may have problems but it is the best system of government. (Agree/Disagree)

In the VOTP survey 2002–2005, the results for both items showed that a majority of respondents were, in general, satisfied with democracy as the best system of government. For the first question, 65 per cent of the global respondents were satisfied with democracy. The second question showed that 79 per cent of the global respondents believed that democracy was the best system of government. Again, as in the WVS, it seems that a majority of the global population were in broad support of democracy. These survey items also illustrate the broad approach to measuring overall global support for democracy. The results of the 2002–2005 VOTP survey can be seen in the two graphs that follow (Figures 3.1 and 3.2).

Regional research projects

As stated earlier, there are also a number of regional projects that gather data similar to that gathered in the WVS, but they are more specific to a region. In this section, questions about democracy from a number of these projects are inspected. One should note again that only certain general questions about democracy are selected and that these surveys contained many more in-depth questions that fall outside the scope of this investigation.

DOI: 10.1057/9781137496195.0008

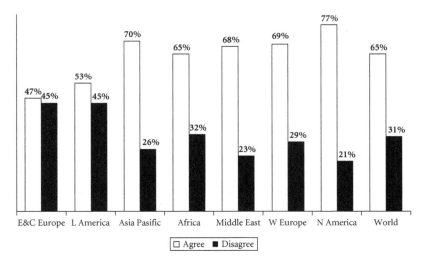

FIGURE 3.1   *VOTP survey: global satisfaction with democracy*

Source: Voice of the people.

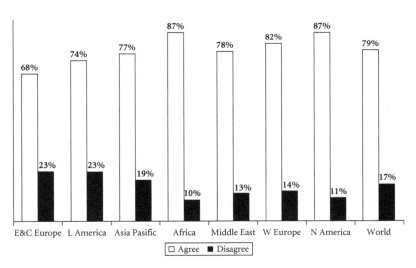

FIGURE 3.2   *VOTP survey: global sentiment on democracy*

Source: Voice of the people.

DOI: 10.1057/9781137496195.0008

AfroBarometer

The first regional study of interest is the AfroBarometer. This study by the Institute for Democracy in South Africa (IDASA), in partnership with the Ghana Centre for Democratic Development (GCDD) and the Department of Political Science at Michigan State University, measures public attitudes on democracy, markets, civil society, and other aspects of development.[20] There have been five rounds of this programme, the most recent of which was the 2011–2013 wave. In the earlier 2008–2009 wave of the survey, which was used for this study's analysis, 26,414 respondents from 20 African countries answered various questions. The responses can be seen in Tables 3.3–3.5. The first question relevant to democracy was as follows:

> *Q30. Which of these three statements is closest to your own opinion?*

From this question one can see that 75.6 per cent of the respondents from the 20 African countries preferred democracy. As with the results from the global level programmes mentioned earlier, there again seemed to be a strong broad support for democracy. The response to another closely related question seeking the respondents' opinion can be seen in Table 3.4. The question was:

> *Q42a. In your opinion, how much of a democracy is [country] today?*

TABLE 3.3   *AfroBarometer: question 30 – support for democracy*

		Total
Q30. Support for democracy	Missing	0.0%
	Statement 3: It doesn't matter	12.6%
	Statement 2: Sometimes non-democratic preferable	11.8%
	Statement 1: Democracy is preferable	75.6%
	Total	22,127 (100%)

Source: AfroBarometer.[21]

TABLE 3.4   *AfroBarometer: question 42a – extent of democracy*

		Total
Q42a: Extent of democracy in own country	Missing	0.10%
	Not a democracy	6.90%
	A democracy, with major problems	27.50%
	A democracy, but with minor problems	31.50%
	A full democracy	29.20%
	Do not understand question/democracy	4.80%
	Total	22,474 (100%)

Source: AfroBarometer.

DOI: 10.1057/9781137496195.0008

TABLE 3.5   *AfroBarometer: question 43 – satisfaction with democracy*

		Total
Q43: Satisfaction with democracy in own country	Missing	0.10%
	Not a democracy	1.50%
	Not at all satisfied	18.50%
	Not very satisfied	26.50%
	Fairly satisfied	30.20%
	Very satisfied	23.10%
	Total	21,963 (100%)

Source: AfroBarometer.

Another, more probing question was:

> *Q43. Overall, how satisfied are you with the way democracy works in [country]?*

Both questions Q42a and Q43 (Tables 3.4 and 3.5) focussed on African opinions on democracy with Q42a (Table 3.4) showing that 65.90 per cent of the respondents felt that they were either not living in a democracy, or that there were some problems with the democracy within which they lived. The responses to the question Q43 (Table 3.5), showed that about 45 per cent of the respondents were 'not at all' or 'not very satisfied' with democracy compared to 53.30 per cent that were 'fairly' or 'very satisfied'. The results of both these questions highlighted the fact that even though the respondents were broadly supportive of democracy (as explained by Q30 in Table 3.3 earlier), there were strong issues with the functioning of democracy and fairly high levels of dissatisfaction. Although many respondents pay positive lip service to democracy as a whole, the concern lies with the negative sentiment that seems to be present when considering the functioning of democracy. It is, therefore, this type of question that brings us even closer to finding the relevant approach to measuring democracy with the methods developed in this book.

LatinoBarometer (Latinobarómetro)

The LatinoBarometer is similar to the AfroBarometer, except that it examines attitudes from respondents from 18 Latin American countries. The 2010 wave of this survey included similar questions to that of the AfroBarometer 2008–2009 wave, as can be seen in Tables 3.6–3.8.[22]

> *A101. Which of these three statements is closest to your own opinion?*

DOI: 10.1057/9781137496195.0008

TABLE 3.6   *LatinoBarometer: question A101 – support for democracy*

		Total
A101: Support for democracy	Democracy is preferable to any other form of government	68.00%
	In some circumstances, an authoritarian government can be preferable	15.30%
	People like me do not care about being democratic	16.80%
	Total	21,117 (100%)

Source: LatinoBarometer.

TABLE 3.7   *LatinoBarometer: question A107 – democracy as system of governance*

		Total
A107: Democracy may have problems, but it is the best system of government	Strongly agree	29.70%
	Agree	53.30%
	Disagree	14.10%
	Strongly disagree	2.90%
	Total	21,325 (100%)

Source: LatinoBarometer.

TABLE 3.8   *LatinoBarometer: question A102 – satisfaction with democracy*

		Total
A102: Satisfaction with how democracy works in own country	Very satisfied	10.00%
	Fairly satisfied	36.20%
	Not very satisfied	38.80%
	Not at all satisfied	15.10%
	Total	21,117 (100%)

Source: LatinoBarometer.

A107. Democracy may have problems, but it is the best system of government.

In these questions of the LatinoBarometer, 68 per cent of the respondents stated that democracy was preferable to any other form of government. A further 83 per cent of respondents 'agree' or 'strongly agree' that even though democracy might have problems, it still was the best system of government. Again, as with the previous studies, one can see the broad support of democracy as a form of government.

Question A102, however, again highlighted the fact that there are problems in the functioning of democracy, since 53.9 per cent of the respondents were 'not very' or 'not satisfied at all' with democracy

DOI: 10.1057/9781137496195.0008

in their countries. Here again is the type of question that can be supplemented by data gathered with the methodology we present in Chapter 4.

> A102. *In general, would you say you are very satisfied, not satisfied with the way democracy works in [country]?*

The result was as shown in Table 3.8.

The LatinoBarometer contains a total of 50 questions relating to democracy. Some of the more relevant questions, not to be discussed in detail, besides the ones discussed earlier, were:

▸ A108: Democracy is the only system that (country) can be developed.
▸ A109: Democracy is indispensable to become a developed country.
▸ A110: Would you be willing to defend democracy when it is threatened?
▸ A111: Trust in democracy as a system of government for their country to become a developed country.

There are various other research projects looking at opinions on democracy, *inter alia*, the ArabBarometer, the European Values Study, the NCCR Democracy Barometer,[23] the EuroBarometer,[24] the New Russia Barometer,[25] the Korea Barometer,[26] the Democracy Barometer[27] and so on. These are examples of projects that broadly use similar methods of survey research to gauge broad public expressions. What these programmes and those examined earlier have in common is more than the measurement of democracy – they all used survey data in the form of questionnaires with rigid, uniform survey items, so as to gain standardised information.

The strength of the survey data for democratic measurement is that it attempts to provide equal consideration to all opinions.[28] However, survey data measurement can be tedious and expensive to gather. There are also a number of other problems with this method, such as the social and psychological pressures that were placed on respondents of the questionnaires.[29] Survey data, therefore, is not seen as a tool that provides perfectly objective and perfectly efficient measurements of public expressions. This is problematic because, as noted earlier, it is paramount to the functioning of democracy to understand mass attitudes on the subject. The field can, therefore, benefit from more efficient tools to expand on the traditional measuring techniques.

DOI: 10.1057/9781137496195.0008

Twitter as a new public sphere

Rich data sources already exist to extend the value of the traditional survey-based research for alternative sources of opinion. Instead of actively collecting specific data from questionnaires, one can analyse data that is publicly available to extend specific insights. Social media provides a valuable source for opinion-rich data as it contains, *inter alia*, ever-growing, up-to-date streams of short messages, longer blogs, images and videos. These opinion-rich sources come from an increasing variety of users and although this group of users do not (yet) represent the fullness of society, it can at least give one a glimpse of a specific influential sector of society.

Our analysis of social media does not need to replace traditional methods of measuring expressions on democracy, but it could supplement the data gathered by traditional methods. This can provide a deeper understanding of opinions from a specific section of the population, namely, the Internet users or, as they are commonly called, the 'netizens'. At present, this section of society consists largely of the young, and they are, arguably, one of the most influential sectors in the society with the potential to bring (or at least instigate and promote) revolutionary change to the larger population. It is these netizens who have been instrumental in recent large political upheavals, such as the so-called Arab Spring; the 2013–2014 Ukrainian civil unrest; and the ongoing socio-economically driven political unrest in Chile, Argentina, Brazil, Venezuela, Thailand and many other countries across the globe. Individuals such as Wael Ghonim (2011), who effectively used his Facebook page, 'We are Khaled Said', to organise mass regime-changing protests in Egypt, epitomise the effect this sector of society can have: young netizens are often the organisers and instigators of large civil events. They use Facebook, Twitter, blogs and the thousands of other digital channels available to them, and they express their opinions on everything from the latest fashion trends to foreign policy and expressions on democracy. Their thoughts, beliefs and expressions are for the whole world to see and for researchers to analyse.

The question now becomes whether Twitter would be able to provide additional insights to the aforementioned projects measuring democracy. This book examines Twitter using the broad theoretical perspectives of the German sociologist and philosopher Jürgen Habermas and treats expressions on Twitter as a form of discourse within a Habermasian[30]

DOI: 10.1057/9781137496195.0008

public sphere. Scholars such as Habermas[31] and Hannah Arendt[32] have discussed the public sphere and how this sphere is constantly changing. Habermas[33] has looked specifically at the influence of the media on political opinion in the public sphere.

The public sphere refers to a place, be it physical or virtual, where citizens gather and exchange views on public affairs. These spheres are 'places' where citizens can meet and discuss, debate and deliberate on current affairs which eventually leads to the formation of public opinion.[34] The contemporary view of the public sphere is mainly based on the works of Habermas.[35] He defines the public sphere as a 'network for communicating information and points of view...filtered and synthesized in such a way that they coalesce into bundles of topically specified public opinions'.[36]

The public sphere is a normative idea as it is an ideal for good and accountable governance. The rationale is that if a state has a well-functioning and democratic public sphere, then citizens would, in a participatory fashion, assert their influence on political decisions and hold governments responsible.[37] According to Habermas[38] a crisis of legitimacy could develop if the citizens feel that they are not being recognised in the institutions of society. This, in turn, could lead to a crisis of authority and culminate in a re-definition of power relationships within a state.[39]

Throughout the development of democracy there have been many versions of public spheres promoting political accountability. Some examples are the *agora* of Greek City States, where citizens gathered and discussed public affairs. Another form would be the tribal gatherings and certain church congregations throughout history. In European monarchies the royal court was also a public sphere, but it was dominated by the monarch. During the seventeenth and eighteenth centuries, salons (France), coffeehouses (England) and table societies (Germany) were public spheres that were limited to the aristocracy. As technology developed and mass newspapers became distributed, the discussions from these coffeehouses and salons became truly public.[40]

Today, with the rapid development of technology, there are those[41] who argue that new forms of public spheres are developing with the help of information and communication technologies. This means people no longer have to gather physically to discuss public affairs.

Using the ideas from Habermas,[42] a number of scholars such as Papacharissi[43] have examined social media sites and the Internet as new

DOI: 10.1057/9781137496195.0008

types of public spheres where public opinion is being generated and discussed. The creator of Twitter, Jack Dorsey, stated at the 2012 Digital Life Design Conference in Munich that Twitter is a public medium that hosts public conversation in a way simple enough for anyone to use.[44] If this statement is an accurate representation of Twitter, the discussions on Twitter might be comparable to a type of Habermasian public sphere, and the opinions generated here can be of the utmost value in gauging public opinion. The expressions on democracy from this sphere could then be indicative of the legitimacy of democracy as a whole.[45]

Authors such as Carey,[46] Habermas[47] and Papacharissi[48] have argued that the commercialised mass media have created a public space rather than a healthy public sphere. They also contend that in this public space the rhetoric and objectives of the media are colonised by capitalist interests.

The question can now be asked whether Twitter would fall under the category of public space or a public sphere. In the public space, social matters might be discussed, but they would not necessarily lead to the formation of public opinion that could potentially award legitimacy to specific state institutions in a democracy, as would happen in a Habermasian[49] public sphere. However, it should be noted that the view that mass media, including Twitter, can be seen as a form of public sphere is not held by all academics. Some argue that a public sphere is more than just a public space as a healthy public sphere should function independently from the state and/or the economy.[50] Furthermore, it should facilitate rational discourse on public affairs directed towards the common good.

Using the ideas from Habermas, a number of scholars such as Papacharissi,[51] Castells,[52] Downey and Fenton,[53] Dahlberg,[54] Trenz[55] and Gruicic[56] have examined the Internet as a new type of public sphere. At present there is no significant formal study that has examined whether Twitter can, in fact, be fully classified as a public sphere. There are informal articles such as those by Sluis,[57] Hauth,[58] Clemens[59] and Neal[60] that express a range of views on this question. However, most of these articles conclude that it is unclear whether Twitter at present is a healthy public sphere. The closest analysis of new media and the Internet as a form of public sphere can be found in the works of Zizi Papacharissi[61] and Downey and Fenton.[62]

Downey and Fenton[63] have stated that public discussion on new media sites might lead to the creation of counter-public spheres, which could challenge the opinions of the current public sphere. This idea of

DOI: 10.1057/9781137496195.0008

counter-public spheres was developed by Habermas[64] when he recognised that alternative public spheres might challenge the current dominant sphere. This might also be the case for Twitter, but we are of the opinion that expressions on Twitter would rather form part of the dominant public sphere. This, however, remains to be tested in future studies.

In her book *A Private Sphere: Democracy in a Digital Age*, Papacharissi[65] has argued that new technologies have, in fact, eroded the boundaries between the private and the public sphere. She believes that the public sphere is no longer the centre of democratic debate and that private citizens now broadcast gestures of a social, civic, political, cultural and economic nature from the mobile enclosures of the private sphere to mass global audiences. She also believes that these spheres are not fully public as there is an unfair distribution of access to information, a lack of reciprocity in communication and an overarching commercialisation that inhibits open discussion. Papacharissi, therefore, would rather explain expressions on new media as falling within the private sphere.

As yet, there is no definitive answer to whether Twitter can be seen as a Habermasian public sphere in which public opinion can be created. In this study it will, however, be accepted that Twitter does indeed meet the criteria of a public sphere. The expressions measured in this study would, therefore, form part of the discussion that influences the formation of public opinion.

What we do point out now already is that views expressed on Twitter do not necessarily 'coalesce into bundles of topically specified public opinions' as required by the Habermasian definition of the public sphere. For this process of coalescence to emerge, new methodologies of aggregation of data are needed.

Emerging methods of measuring public expression

In recent years, there has been an eruption of opinion mining and sentiment analysis with all the new ways of gauging public opinion other than the traditional research projects described earlier. This is owing to the increasing availability of opinion-rich resources – specifically online sources.[66] Consequently, the development of automated computerised methods of analysing Big Data online has given birth to a new generation of studies on public expression. These studies can be broadly grouped into those that aim to predict future events and those that aim to explain

DOI: 10.1057/9781137496195.0008

or describe the present by using data from online sources. The method developed in this book falls into the latter category.

The prediction studies, also referred to as forecasting studies, have aimed broadly to predict the future using Big Data from various sources. An example of a recent predictive study using social media is the 2010 *Computers and Society* article by Asur and Huberman 'Predicting the Future with Social Media'.[67] This study stated that although social media is becoming ubiquitous, the content generated from these websites remains largely untapped. With a specific focus on Twitter they demonstrated 'how social media content can be used to predict real-world outcomes'. By using Twitter data to forecast box-office revenues for movies they illustrated that 'a simple model built from the rate at which Tweets are created about particular topics can outperform market-based predictors'.[68] They further showed that statements taken from Twitter can be used to improve the predicting power of social media.

Other researchers have tried to predict specific events such as changes in the stock market,[69] elections[70] and even medical emergencies such as a Swine Flu pandemic.[71] In the field of political risk analysis, a rising data scientist from RPX Corporation, Jay Yonamine,[72] has published numerous studies on forecasting various forms of conflict using machine-learning techniques in combination with open-source data, including data from social media networks. In his paper 'Using GDELT to Forecast Violence in Afghanistan'[73] Yonamine attempted to predict future levels of violence in Afghanistan districts by using open source, machine-coded event data for Afghanistan with GDELT (Global Dataset of Events, Location and Tone) to build temporally and geo-spatially nuanced forecasts of political violence. He used the GDELT data,[74] which contains over 200 million open-source gathered events that are machine-coded in near real-time. In this paper, he showed that it is at least feasible to build a relatively accurate method that can give nuanced predictions on a sub-state level of violence in Afghanistan. However, authors of these predictive studies all note that the studies are in their infancy and will need much refinement before they can be effective predictors and forecasters of the future. These studies have also received strong criticism from writers such as Gayo-Avello,[75] who stated that (writing in 2012) it is still impossible and futile to attempt a prediction of future events from social media and other forms of open-source data.

This book falls in the second category of studies looking at automated analysis of Big Data from social media sites as a descriptive method. Instead of trying to predict the future, these descriptive studies have

DOI: 10.1057/9781137496195.0008

focused on measuring factors such as public mood, public opinion and various forms of public expressions from social media sites such as Twitter. A brief look at a number of recent influential studies can provide one with a better understanding of this emerging field of research.

One study, such as the 2008 article 'Opinion Mining and Sentiment Analysis' by Pang and Lee,[76] examined various sources of online information that could provide meaningful commercial and political opinions. The authors specifically scrutinised online advice columns, blogs, consumer ratings on commercial sites, discussion forums and social media sites to develop an opinion search application that will automatically 'crawl' through the Internet and extract all relevant opinion data. There are, however, a number of obstacles listed in this study regarding this type of automated extraction application. Most of the obstacles relate to the ability of computers to understand natural (human) language.[77] This is indeed a big obstacle for all analysis on digital data. Although computers and their software are improving at an unprecedented rate, much of the subtle nuances of human language still escape our digital counterparts. Consequently, as natural language-processing software and machine learning improves, so can the analysis of human-generated digital content improve.

Although Twitter is still young, a big portion of research on measuring public expressions from online sources focusses on data from Twitter. The reason for this, as has been discussed earlier, is that the Twitter information is publicly available, downloadable and contains short concrete sentences which often express sentiment.

One of the earliest studies looking at Tweet data was conducted by Bollen, Pepe and Mao,[78] which attempted to model public mood and emotion using Twitter. The study's aim was to use Tweet data in combination with a psychometric mood measurement instrument to classify the mood of a large number of Tweets. The results of the study showed that real world events such as stock market fluctuations and elections have had an immediate effect on various dimensions of public mood as expressed through Twitter. They speculated that a large-scale analysis of public mood could provide a framework for measuring collective social and emotional trends of specific sections of the population.[79] In a sense this is what this book attempts to accomplish with the methodology for measuring expressions on democracy via Twitter.

It should be noted that most of these descriptive studies were conducted by computer scientists; however, in 2010, Hopkins and King[80] decided to create a method to categorise the large amount of digitally

DOI: 10.1057/9781137496195.0008

created information for measuring sentiment that would be more useful to the social sciences. In their study, they developed a method of automated non-parametric content analysis for social science. This method examined a collection of digitised texts and approximated unbiased estimates of category proportions. The authors also included a coding package[81] that can be used to replicate their results. The incorporation of this automated non-parametric content analysis method can be considered for future research expanding on the work in this book.[82]

As these descriptive studies began to gain traction, more diverse studies were conducted by an ever-growing group of researchers from all academic fields. In 2010, an interesting study by Diakopoulos and Shamma[83] examined the possibility of characterising debate performance from aggregated sentiment expressed on Twitter. They looked specifically at sentiments after televised US presidential debates in 2008. The results of their research showed that sentiments on Twitter favoured Obama over McCain during the debates. They believe that news agencies would benefit from analysing debate results in this manner.

The most significant work with a bearing on this book, however, is an article by O'Connor et al.[84] Their paper, entitled 'From Tweets to Polls: Linking Text Sentiment to Public Opinion Time Series', compared survey data on consumer confidence and political opinion with sentiment-word frequencies in Twitter messages. Therefore, it directly compares survey data to automated Tweet analysis. The study found that there is a strong correlation between the survey and sentiment data; in some cases the correlation was as high as 80 per cent. This study, therefore, showed that it is theoretically possible to supplement, or in some cases even substitute, survey data with sentiment data gathered from Twitter. They further argued that examining public expressions from Twitter to supplement or replace survey data could save money, time and allow one to collect information on a much wider variety of topics. Since our study supports the idea that survey data can be complimented by automated Tweet analysis, it was decided to use their study as the backbone for the operationalisation of this research's methodology.

Conclusion

The relevance of measuring public expressions and opinions on democracy is clear: it has been shown that opinions on democracy are

DOI: 10.1057/9781137496195.0008

paramount to the democratic consolidation and broad functioning of democracy in a country. Considering that opinions on democracy are important, it is understandable that there are many projects attempting to measure these expressions and opinions. It is interesting to note that according to Inglehart,[85] many questions from the different traditional surveys and projects overlap in their use of indicators for democratic support. What is even more relevant to this study is that these surveys contain a high level of internal consistency. What this means is that if a person supports democracy on one of the indicators, they tend to support democracy on the other indicators as well. For this study it would mean that if a person (or Tweet, in this case) shows support for a specific aspect of democracy, there is a high probability that the person would also support other aspects of democracy.

Although great uncertainty still remains whether Twitter and other forms of social media can be seen as a true Habermasian public sphere, this study will treat it as such. As illustrated earlier, a number of novel methods for measuring expressions from online sources have recently emerged. One of these methods, described by O'Connor et al.,[86] will be used as a basis for the method of measuring public expressions on democracy from Twitter that will be developed in the next chapter.

This study's focus on broad levels of support for democracy expressed through positive or negative sentiments in Tweets relating to democracy for the chosen period is only the start. In subsequent studies, the incorporation of data from more social media sites could help focus the research on specific questions instead of broad sentiment. Furthermore, although this study focusses on democracy, these questions could be concerned with any field of research. Their application is therefore essentially only bound by the imagination of the future researcher.

Notes

1   U. Van Beek (2012) 'The Crisis That Shook the World', in U. Van Beek and E. Wnuk-Lipinski (eds), *Democracy under Stress: The Global Crisis and Beyond* (Berlin: Barbara Budrich Publishers), p. 12.

2   D. Lerner (1958) *The Passing of Traditional Society: Modernizing the Middle East* (New York: Free Press); G.A. Almond and S. Verba (1963) *The Civic Culture: Political Attitudes and Democracy in Five Nations* (London: SAGE Publications); H. Eckstein (1966) *Division and Cohesion in Democracy: A Study of Norway* (Princeton, NJ: Princeton University Press); R. Inglehart and

DOI: 10.1057/9781137496195.0008

C. Welzel (2005) *Modernization, Cultural Change, and Democracy: The Human Development Sequence* (Cambridge: Cambridge University Press).

3   M. Castells (2008) 'The New Public Sphere: Global Civil Society, Communication Networks, and Global Governance', *The Annals of the American Academy of Political and Social Science*, 616, 78–94.

4   M. Bratton and R. Mattes (2001) 'Support for Democracy in Africa: Intrinsic or Instrumental?' *British Journal of Political Science*, 31(3), 447–474; L. Diamond (1999) *Developing Democracy: Toward Consolidation* (Maryland: John Hopkins University Press); D.C. Shin (2006) *Democratization: Perspectives from Global Citizenries*. CSD Working Papers. University of California, Irvine: Centre for the Study of Democracy; J. Linz (1990) 'Transitions to Democracy', *Washington Quarterly*, 13, 143–162; R. Rose (2001) 'A Divergent Europe', *Journal of Democracy*, 12(1), 93–106.

5   Diamond, *Developing Democracy*, p. 168; M.D. Fails and H.N. Pierce (2010) 'Changing Mass Attitudes and Democratic Deepening', *Political Research Quarterly*, 63(1), 174–187.

6   Van Beek, 'The Crisis That Shook the World', p. 12.

7   I.L. Horowitz (1991) 'Anti-modernization, National Character and Social Structure', *Journal of Contemporary History*, 26(3/4), 355–367.

8   A. Lijphart (1985) *Democracies* (New Haven, CT: Yale University Press); A. Lijphart (1990) *Democracies: Patterns of Majoritarian and Consensus Government in 22 Countries* (New Haven, CT: Yale University Press).

9   T.D. Sisk (1994) 'Perspectives of South Africa's Transition: Implications for Democratic Consolidation', *Politikon: South African Journal of Political Studies*, 21(1), 66–75.

10 Almond and Verba, *The Civic Culture*.

11 R. Inglehart (2003) 'How Solid Is Mass Support for Democracy: And How Can We Measure It?' *Asian Barometer* (Online, available at: http://www.asianbarometer.org/newenglish/publications/ConferencePapers/2003conference/T_03_no.11.pdf [30/05/2012]).

12 Inglehart, 'How Solid Is Mass Support for Democracy?'

13 R. Rose, W. Mishler and C. Haerpfer (1998) *Democracy and Its Alternatives* (Baltimore, MD: The Johns Hopkins University Press).

14 A. Hadenius and J. Teorell (2006) 'Cultural and Economic Prerequisites of Democracy: Reassessing Recent Evidence', *Studies in Comparative International Development*, 39(4), 87–106; R. Inglehart and C. Welzel (2005) *Modernization, Cultural Change, and Democracy: The Human Development Sequence* (Cambridge: Cambridge University Press); C. Welzel and R. Inglehart (2008) 'The Role of Ordinary People in Democratization', *Journal of Democracy*, 19(1), 126–140; C.H. Knutsen (2010) 'Measuring Effective Democracy', *International Political Science Review*, 31(2), 109–128.

DOI: 10.1057/9781137496195.0008

15   WVS (2012) *World Values Survey: The World's Most Comprehensive Investigation of Political and Sociocultural Change* (Online, available at: http://www. worldvaluessurvey.org/ [17/06/2014]).

16   H.E. Brady (2000) 'Contributions of Survey Research to Political Science', *PS: Political Science and Politics*, 33(1), 47–57.

17   Inglehart and Welzel, *Modernization, Cultural Change and Democracy*. See also R. Inglehart (2007) 'Post-materialist Values and the Shift from Survival to Self-Expression Values', in R. Dalton and H.-D. Klingeman (eds), *The Oxford Handbook of Political Behavior* (Oxford: Oxford University Press), pp. 223–239.

18   *World Values Survey*.

19   Voice of the People (2012) *An Annual Worldwide Survey – The Voice of the People* (Online, available at: http://www.voice-of-the-people.net/ [16/08/2012]).

20   AfroBarometer (2008) 'The Quality of Democracy and Governance in Africa: New Results from Afrobarometer Round 4', *Afrobarometer Network*. Working Paper No. 108 (Online, available at: http://www.afrobarometer.org/ files/documents/working_papers/AfropaperNo108.pdf [16/08/2012]).

21   AfroBarometer (2008) *AfroBarometer Online Data Analysis* (Online, available at: http://www.jdsurvey.net/afro/AnalizeSample.jsp [30/05/2012]).

22   LatinoBarometer (2012) *Online Results Analysis* (Online, available at: http:// www.latinobarometro.org/latino/LATAnalizeQuestion.jsp [16/08/2012]).

23   NCCR Democracy (2014) *Democracy Barometer* (Online, available at: http:// www.nccr-democracy.uzh.ch/research/module5/barometer/democracy-barometer-for-established-democracies [23/01/2014]).

24   European Commission (2014) *Eurobarometer* (Online, available at: http:// ec.europa.eu/public_opinion/index_en.htm [23/01/2014]).

25   University of Strathclyde, Glasgow (2014) *New Russia Barometer* (Online, available at: http://www.cspp.strath.ac.uk/catalog1_0.html [23/01/2014]).

26   Kobar (2014) *The Korea Barometer* (Online, available at: http://www. koreabarometer.org/ [23/01/2014]).

27   Democracy Barometer (2014) *Welcome page* (Online, available at: http:// www.democracybarometer.org/ [23/01/2014]).

28   S. Verba (1996) 'The Citizen as Respondent: Sample Surveys and American Democracy', Presidential Address, American Political Science Association, 1995. *American Political Science Review*, 90(1), 1–7.

29   A.J. Berinsky (1999) 'The Two Faces of Public Opinion', *American Journal of Political Science*, 43(4), 1209–1230.

30   J. Habermas (1989) *The Structural Transformation of the Public Sphere: An Inquiry into a Category of Bourgeois Society* (Cambridge: Polity Press).

31   Habermas, *The Structural Transformation of the Public Sphere*.

32   H. Arendt (1963) *On Revolution* (London: Macmillan).

33   Arendt, *On Revolution*.

DOI: 10.1057/9781137496195.0008

34 M. Castells (2008) 'The New Public Sphere: Global Civil Society, Communication Networks, and Global Governance', *The Annals of the American Academy of Political and Social Science*, 616, 78–94.

35 Habermas, *The Structural Transformation of the Public Sphere*.

36 J. Habermas (1996) *Between Fact and Norms* (Cambridge, MA: MIT Press), p. 360.

37 CommGAP (2012) *The Public Sphere*. Communication for Governance and Accountability Program, The World Bank (Online, available at: http://siteresources.worldbank.org/EXTGOVACC/Resources/PubSphereweb.pdf [20/08/2012]).

38 J. Habermas (1976) *Legitimation Crisis* (London: Heinemann).

39 S. Sassen (2006) *Territory, Authority, Rights: From Medieval to Global Assemblages* (Princeton, NJ: Princeton University Press); Castells, 'The New Public Sphere', 80.

40 CommGAP, *The Public Sphere*; Castells, 'The New Public Sphere', 78–94.

41 Such as Castells, 'The New Public Sphere'; Z.A. Papacharissi (2002) 'The Virtual Sphere: The Internet as a Public Sphere', *New Media & Society*, 4(1), 9–27; J. Downey and N. Fenton (2003) 'New Media, Counter Publicity and the Public Sphere', *New Media & Society*, 5(2), 185–202; L. Dahlberg (2001) 'The Internet and Democratic Discourse: Exploring the Prospects of Online Deliberative Forums Extending the Public Sphere', *Information, Communication & Society*, 4(4), 615–633; M.D. Gruicic (2011) 'Internet and the Structural Transformation of Public Debate – A Comparison of the Online and Offline Public Spheres in Croatia', master's thesis. Central European University; H. Trenz (2009) *Digital Media and the Return of the Representative Public Sphere*. Working Paper. Centre for European Studies.

42 Habermas, *The Structural Transformation of the Public Sphere*.

43 Papacharissi, 'The Virtual Sphere 2.0'.

44 VentureBeat (2012) 'Jack Dorsey: Twitter Seeing 3 to 5 Percent Engagement on Promoted TweetTweets and Trends', *Venture Beat News* (Online, available at: http://venturebeat.com/2012/01/22/jack-dorsey-promoted-products/#vGidIvFfak4DDYXQ.99 [30/01/2012]).

45 Habermas, *Legitimation Crisis*; CommGAP, *The Public Sphere*.

46 J.W. Carey (1995) 'The Press, Public Opinion, and Public Discourse', in T.L. Glasser and C.T. Salmon (eds), *Public Opinion and the Communication of Consent* (New York: The Guilford Press), pp. 373–402.

47 Habermas, *Legitimation Crisis*.

48 Z.A. Papacharissi (2010) *A Private Sphere: Democracy in a Digital Age* (Cambridge: Polity Press).

49 Habermas. *Legitimation Crisis*.

DOI: 10.1057/9781137496195.0008

50   N. Garnham (1992) 'The Media and the Public Sphere', in C. Calhoun (ed.), *Habermas and the Public Sphere* (Cambridge, MA: MIT Press), pp. 359–370; Habermas. *Legitimation Crisis*.

51   Papacharissi, 'The Virtual Sphere', 9–27; Papacharissi, *A Private Sphere*.

52   Castells, 'The New Public Sphere', 78–94.

53   Downey and Fenton, 'New Media, Counter Publicity and the Public Sphere', 185–202.

54   Dahlberg (2001) 'The Internet and Democratic Discourse', 615–633.

55   Trenz, *Digital Media and the Return of the Representative Public Sphere*.

56   Gruicic, 'Internet and the Structural Transformation of Public Debate'.

57   E. Sluis (2009) 'Twitter: Public Space or Public Sphere?' *Masters of Media* (Online, available at: http://mastersofmedia.hum.uva.nl/2009/10/06/twitter-public-space-or-public-sphere/ [20/08/2012]).

58   A. Hauth (2010) 'Twitter as a Public Sphere', *New Media and Democracy* (Online, available at: http://www.personal.psu.edu/alh5147/blogs/cas497a/2010/02/twitter-as-a-public-sphere.html [20/08/2012]).

59   R. Clemens (2012) 'Twitter as a Public Sphere?' *21st Century Scholar* (Online, available at: http://21stcenturyscholar.org/2012/06/05/twitter-as-a-public-sphere/ [20/08/2012]).

60   C. Neal (2012) 'The Public Sphere and the New Media', *Social Media Today* (Online, available at: http://socialmediatoday.com/node/495708&utm_source=feedburner_twitter&utm_medium=twitter&utm_campaign=autotweettweets [20/08/2012]).

61   Papacharissi, 'The Virtual Sphere', 9–27; Papacharissi, *A Private Sphere*. Plato, *The Republic*.

62   Downey and Fenton, 'New Media, Counter Publicity and the Public Sphere', pp. 185–202.

63   Downey and Fenton, 'New Media, Counter Publicity and the Public Sphere', p. 200.

64   J. Habermas (1992) *Between Fact and Norms* (Cambridge, MA: MIT Press), p. 427.

65   Papacharissi, *A Private Sphere*; Plato, *The Republic*.

66   B. Pang and L. Lee (2008) 'Opinion Mining and Sentiment Analysis', *Foundations and Trends in Information Retrieval*, 2(1/2), 1–135.

67   S. Asur and B.A. Huberman (2010) 'Predicting the Future with Social Media', *Computers and Society*. Cornell University Computer Science Paper.

68   Asur and Huberman, 'Predicting the Future with Social Media'.

69   J. Bollen, H. Mao and X. Zeng (2011) 'Twitter Mood Predicts the Stock Market', *Journal of Computational Science*, 2(1), 1–8.

70   R. Lindsay (2008) *Predicting Polls with Lexicon* (Online, available at: http://languagewrong.tumblr.com/post/55722687/predicting-polls-with-lexicon [25/07/2012]); A. Tumasjan et al. (2010) *Predicting Elections with Twitter: What 140 Characters Reveal about Political Sentiment*. Proceedings of the Fourth

DOI: 10.1057/9781137496195.0008

International AAAI Conference on Weblogs and Social Media. Technische Universität München; D. Gayo-Avello (2012) 'I Wanted to Predict Elections with Twitter and All I Got Was This Lousy Paper: A Balanced Survey on Election Prediction Using Twitter Data', *Computers and Society*. Cornell University Computer Science Paper.

71 J. Ritterman, M. Osborne and E. Klein (2009) *Using Prediction Markets and Twitter to Predict a Swine Flu Pandemic*. University of Edinburgh (Online, available at: http://homepages.inf.ed.ac.uk/miles/papers/swine09.pdf [09/08/2012]).

72 J. Yonamine (2013) *Using GDELT to Forecast Violence in Afghanistan* (Online, available at: http://jayyonamine.com/?p=645 [09/07/2014]).

73 Yonamine, *Using GDELT to Forecast Violence in Afghanistan*.

74 The GDELT Project (2014) *Watching Our World Unfold* (Online, available at: http://gdeltproject.org/ [09/07/2014]).

75 Gayo-Avello, 'I Wanted to Predict Elections with Twitter and All I Got Was This Lousy Paper'.

76 Pang and Lee, 'Opinion Mining and Sentiment Analysis', 1–135.

77 Pang and Lee, 'Opinion Mining and Sentiment Analysis'.

78 J. Bollen, A. Pepe and H. Mao (2011) *Modelling Public Mood and Emotion: Twitter Sentiment and Socio-economic Phenomena*. In Proceedings of the Fifth International AAAI Conference on Weblogs and Social Media (ICWSM 2011), Barcelona, Spain.

79 Bollen, Pepe and Mao, *Modelling Public Mood and Emotion*.

80 D.J. Hopkins and G. King (2010) 'A Method of Automated Nonparametric Content Analysis for Social Science', *American Journal of Political Science*, 54(1), 229–247.

81 D. Hopkins and G. King (2009) *Replication Data for a Method of Automated Nonparametric Content Analysis for Social Science* (Online, available at: UNF:3: xlE5stLgKvpeMvxzlLxzEQ==hdl:1902.1/12898 [22/02/ 2012]).

82 Hopkins and King's methodology was excluded in this study as a different commercial data processing platform was chosen for our analysis.

83 N.A. Diakopoulos and D.A. Shamma (2010) *Characterizing Debate Performance via Aggregated Twitter Sentiment*. CHI 2010: Proceedings of the 28th International Conference on Human Factors in Computing Systems, 1195–1198.

84 B. O'Connor et al. (2010) 'From TweetTweets to Polls: Linking Text Sentiment to Public Opinion Time Series', in Proceedings of ICWSM: Carnegie Mellon University.

85 Inglehart, 'How Solid Is Mass Support for Democracy: And How Can We Measure It'.

86 O'Connor et al., 'From TweetTweets to Polls'.

DOI: 10.1057/9781137496195.0008

4

Measuring Support for Democracy on Twitter

Abstract: *The broad goal of this chapter is to develop, run and provide the results of the specific research procedures (operations) that will result in empirical observations for measuring public expressions on democracy from Twitter. This analysis attempts to show the extent to which one can measure public expressions on democracy from interest-articulated sentiments gathered from a sample of 'Tweets', processed with content analysis and sentiment analysis software. The second section of this chapter contains the actual measurement of public expressions on democracy from interest-articulated sentiments gathered from a sample of 'Tweets', processed with content analysis and sentiment analysis software for the period of 1 May to 31 July 2012. The third section of this chapter examines the criterion validity of the content analysis and sentiment analysis software used in measuring public expressions on democracy.*

Keywords: commercial data processing platform; content analysis; criterion validity; negative sentiment; positive sentiment; sentiment analysis; Twitter

Lutz, Barend and Pierre du Toit. *Defining Democracy in a Digital Age: Political Support on Social Media.* Basingstoke: Palgrave Macmillan, 2014. DOI: 10.1057/9781137496195.0009.

The broad goal of this chapter is to develop, execute and provide results of the specific research procedures from Twitter that will result in empirical observations for measuring public expressions on democracy. This analysis attempts to show the extent to which one can measure public expressions on democracy from interest-articulated sentiments gathered from a sample of Tweets processed with content and sentiment analysis software. In this section the measurement instrument of our selected commercial data processing platform is examined.[1] The rationale for the choice, function and limitations of this platform are also discussed.

The second section of this chapter contains the actual measurement of public expressions on democracy from interest-articulated sentiments gathered from a sample of Tweets, processed with content analysis and sentiment analysis software. This section relates to the question on measuring public expressions on democracy from the period of 1 May to 31 July 2012.

The third section of this chapter examines the question of the accuracy of content analysis and sentiment analysis software used in measuring the public expressions on democracy from Twitter in the same period. In this section we also do a manual assessment of the classification results produced by the data processing platform.

Following these three sections, a section on the broad relevance of these findings can be found. There are also a number of other interesting findings that have emerged from this study which will be briefly examined as this study has the potential to open up the field of automated measurement of public expressions from online textual data. This final section, therefore, examines potential routes that future research can pursue within this novel field.

Operationalisation

In measuring and analysing expressions on democracy from Twitter and other forms of digital media there are two general routes that can be taken. Firstly, a researcher, organisation or company can collect open source digital data on their own and analyse the collected data with their own analysis methodology and software. This method has been followed in studies such as O'Connor et al.[2] and Hopkins and King[3] where the researchers have privately collected large sets of data and developed methods to analyse these datasets. This method is effective and has

DOI: 10.1057/9781137496195.0009

advantages such as extensive adjustability of the software and collection methodology. However, as this method is extremely time consuming and requires extensive programming and expertise in statistical analysis, there is also a second method that attempts to piggyback on existing infrastructure in an effort to streamline the process and make the approach more accessible. This is the method chosen for this study. In this section the operationalisation of this methodology is discussed.

Multiple digital-media analysis companies focus on collecting and analysing digital content. Many of these companies have 'listening' software that constantly monitors online activity and collects digital information such as Tweets, blogs, comments on company and news sites and various other forms of digital communication. These collected datasets are teeming with information, which is then analysed using each company's specific methodology. The methodologies vary greatly in complexity and scope, but all strive to extract useful information from the collected datasets. This information can be anything from the sentiments of a certain sector of the market on a specific brand to user engagement on quality for a specific news article. Most of these companies focus on market-related analysis, but the data they collect and their analytical methods can be extended to many other fields of research, as will be shown in this chapter.

There are thousands of these companies globally as most large marketing agencies have digital-media analysis divisions, and more of these companies and divisions are emerging every day. This variety gives researchers a line-up of choices when it comes to collecting and analysing digital media. Instead of 're-inventing the wheel', we decided to outsource data collection and analysis to one of the many commercial options available. Some of the larger companies focus specifically on social media analytics such as Brandwatch, Meltwater, 33Across, Hootsuite and Buffer. The emerging companies that were considered for this study included BrandsEye, DataSift and ViralHeat. With this type of commercial platform the user needs minimal computer skills as he/she is only required to enter the specific parameters, such as keywords, which the platform can then use in its automated data collection and analysis.

The measuring instrument: data processing platform

After considering the available commercial options, a specific data processing platform was selected. In October 2011, the company opened

Beta Signup to its analysis platform and invited partners to join collaborative case studies using its platform. This was just in time for our study's initial planning phase as this platform allowed users to gather Tweet data on specific keywords and then use data and sentiment analysis software to analyse and present the processed data. After extensive and extremely insightful correspondence with a prominent developer it was decided to use this analytical platform and sign up for the beta trial in March 2012. However, it should be noted for future studies that a combination of commercial options could be considered to further improve the robustness of the test.

Of paramount importance for this study was the specific function of the data processing platform to enable researchers to export all the Tweets that have been gathered into a Microsoft Excel file. This file contains: (i) the exact date and time each Tweet was created; (ii) all the collected Tweet texts for the chosen period; (iii) the user's Twitter handle (name); (iv) a sentiment score of +1 for positive and −1 for negative for each Tweet; and (v) a detailed decimal sentiment value ranging from −1 to +1. This allowed the researchers to see exactly how positive or how negative the platform has classified a specific Tweet. The example in Table 4.1 shows a Tweet on democracy that has been classified with a negative sentiment value (−0.68094) by the data processing platform.

A sentiment analysis programme, or 'Sentiment Analyser' such as the one contained in this platform, contains a library of positive and negative words which it uses to look for corresponding positive or negative words in each Tweet.[4] The full process of automated sentiment analysis is, however, much more complex, but it falls outside the scope of this study to examine this entire process.[5] What is important to know is that, according to the data processing platform, the Tweet has been classified as approximately 68 per cent negative.

TABLE 4.1   *Sentiment-classified Tweet*

Creation Date	Text	From (User)	Sentiment Label	Sentiment Value
8/12/2012 9:48	America is really bad at democracy. http://t.co/i8nmPjdU	wellslawoffice	−1	−0.68094

Source: Authors' own compilation with data from Twitter.

DOI: 10.1057/9781137496195.0009

Public expressions

After the collection and analytical method was chosen, it was then decided what specific Tweet data was required to enable the system to collect and measure 'public expressions' on democracy. The actual measurement method will be discussed in more detail in the following sub-sections, but the result of this measurement was intended to provide aggregate levels of positive and negative sentiments for the chosen period as two separate percentage scores. The first percentage represented the aggregated score for positive sentiment within the population of Tweets; the second is similar for negative sentiments of Tweets to enable an assessment of what percentage of the total Tweets was classified one way or the other.

As the data processing platform was still in beta testing when this study was conducted, and this was the first time anyone has attempted to measure expressions on democracy from Twitter, it was also important to establish the validity of the content analysis and sentiment analysis on the specific dataset. To do this, a simple random sample (stratified by positive and negative sentiment of Tweets from the population) was selected and manually classified for sentiment. This study has, therefore, within the statistical limitations, attempted to provide an estimate of the criterion validity of the platform as a measuring instrument of sentiment on expressions about democracy on Twitter.

Sentiment classification

Our operationalisation of sentiment classification is based on the O'Connor et al.[6] study discussed in the previous chapter. This study used one billion Tweets for the two-year period 2008–2009. No attempt was made to identify user location or language, but the researchers of the mentioned study acknowledged that better stratified data would provide even more relevant results, although they did not feel that their exploratory study necessitated further analysis.

A similar approach was taken here for this present study as the results were not stratified according to location. This study will, therefore, be representative of only the collected Tweets rather than to give a complete picture of all the expressions on democracy on Twitter. A much larger study will be needed to form such a representation. The goal of this study then, was to illustrate the concept of measuring democracy on Twitter and to establish the effectiveness of the measuring method.

DOI: 10.1057/9781137496195.0009

It was noted that Tweets from O'Connor et al.'s study were processed in a number of ways. Firstly, topical keywords were extracted manually to represent specific issues such as 'consumer confidence', 'elections' and 'presidential approval' (e.g., with 'consumer confidence' the topical words 'economy', 'jobs' and 'job' were chosen). This same manual selection method has been implemented in this study. A number of colloquial versions of the word 'democracy' were chosen to identify Tweets relating specifically to democracy as follows:[7]

> Democracy, democracy, Liberal Democracy, Discursive Democracy, Pluralist Democracy, deliberative democracy, social democracy, demockerycy, deMockracy, democratees, democrabeep, democrackcy, democrack, democrap, democrapsy, democrASS, D3mocr@cy, plutocracy, demo-crazy.

After extracting topical Tweets, the next step needed was for the data to be classified according to sentiment scores. This indicated whether a Tweet expressed a more negative or a more positive sentiment. In the O'Connor et al. study a subjectivity lexicon from OpinionFinder was used to train a Sentiment Analysis programme to extract sentiment from the Tweets. This type of natural language processing is still quite a noisy[8] instrument of measurement, but O'Connor et al.[9] stated that as they are only interested in aggregate sentiment and have so many data points, the errors will mostly cancel each other out. For this study, however, the data processing platform provided sentiment analysis through its online platform.

Data collection

As with the data analysis, there are a number of methods for collecting Tweet data. Firstly, an individual can get access to the Twitter Firehose stream and examine up to 1 per cent of all created Tweets per processing second. To do this one would need a persistent Hypertext Transfer Protocol (HTTP) connection to the low latency connection of Twitter's global stream.[10] This gives an uninterrupted connection to the Internet for the chosen timeframe. Secondly, the process can use dedicated platforms such as the platform we use to collect and analyse the Tweet data. As explained earlier it was deemed unnecessary for this study to streamline the process as the dedicated platforms were sufficient.

Without an over-elaboration of technical details, the Twitter stream Application Programming Interface (API) allows access to 'streams' of public data flowing through Twitter. This is done by accessing what Twitter calls 'the Public Firehose'. However, at the time this study was

DOI: 10.1057/9781137496195.0009

conducted, Twitter limited public access to the Firehose stream to the first 1 per cent of the available Tweets at any given moment so making it possible to view and analyse 1 per cent of the publicly generated Tweets every 'streaming second' into a database.[11] This is commonly called 'Twitter data mining'. It may be necessary to mention here that there are companies such as DataSift, Collecta, CrowdEye, Tap11 and, of course, Twitter that have access to the full Firehose stream. DataSift can even provide a full historic set of Tweets dating back to January 2010.[12] The 1 per cent sample publicly available was, however, sufficient for this introductory methodological and descriptive study.

Figure 4.1 provides a diagram of how the data analysis method functions. As discussed earlier, the study only focused on: (i) 1 per cent of all Tweets that were available for the period. Then from this 1 per cent, all the English language Tweets (ii) which pertained to democracy (iii). These Tweets were then split into those that contained positive sentiments on democracy (iv) and those that contained negative sentiments (v). A neutral section was also finally added (vi) to represent Tweets that have been collected but that did not contain direct sentiment on democracy.

The automatic Tweet collation software was activated to collect the Tweets for the chosen period of collection from 1 May to 31 July 2012.

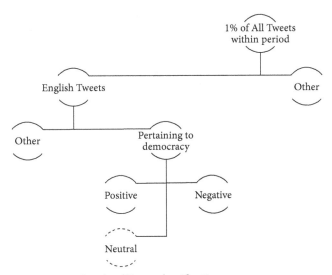

FIGURE 4.1 *Levels of Tweet classification*

Source: Authors' own compilation.

DOI: 10.1057/9781137496195.0009

The first step was to enter the keywords chosen for the platform to search Twitter Firehose to collect Tweets containing these words, after which the data processing platform began its collection and analysis process. The platform then collected 104,037 Tweets which meant that this study now had 104,037 units of analysis relating to democracy.

Representation of measured expressions on democracy from Twitter

There are a number of ways in which this collected data can be represented and we had to find the most appropriate method of presenting the analysed data for this study. Some of the methods used are examined here.

Firstly, a histogram of sentiment classification for the full period of this study was presented in a graph as shown (Figure 4.2). The histogram is broken into 0.025 sentiment increments. On the left of the graph one can see the negative sentiment and on the right the positive sentiment. It was noted that the platform classified more Tweets in the positive range than in the negative range. At first glance it would, therefore, seem that, according to the data processing platform the majority of public expressions on democracy for the chosen period had a positive sentiment. However, this is not necessarily the case, as will be explained in the subsequent section on the criterion validity of the platform as a measuring instrument.

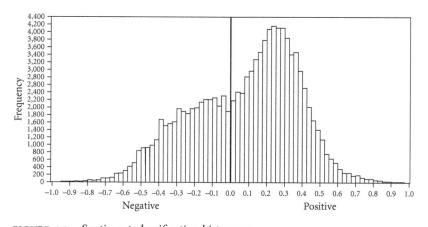

FIGURE 4.2   *Sentiment-classification histogram*

Source: Authors' own compilation, derived from collected data.

DOI: 10.1057/9781137496195.0009

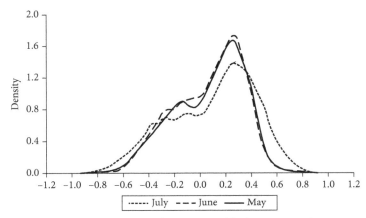

FIGURE 4.3 *Sentiment-classification monthly density spread*
Source: Authors' own compilation, derived from collected data.

The second example is represented in Figure 4.3. This shows the density spread of the sentiment for each month of the study. It also should be noted that the shape of each of the three represented months is quite similar. This corresponds with the spread of sentiment represented in the Tweet data for each month. In addition, the two clear peaks in the data should be noted. The smaller peak between −0.3 and −0.1 represents the bulk of the negative sentiment Tweets. The bigger peak around +0.2 represents the bulk of the positive sentiments. The spread of the negative Tweets, as seen in both Figures 4.3 and 4.4, are broader than the spread of the positive Tweets. This indicates that a wider variety of negative classified Tweets rather than positive Tweets was classified. This fact led to a closer examination of the sentiment classification to understand whether the shape of these graphs could be explained by the data or whether it was something in the data processing platform programming that caused this spread. The findings on the analysis of the accuracy of the measuring instrument will be discussed fully in the next section, but it should be noted here that the shape was, in fact, explained by the programming and not only by the data.

Another informative way of representing the sentiment data of the total 104,037 Tweets is with a scatter graph as in Figure 4.4. This graph, covering the full period of this study, shows the sentiment of each Tweet – represented the set of dots on the left for positive and those on the right for negative. A 250 point moving average line has been added

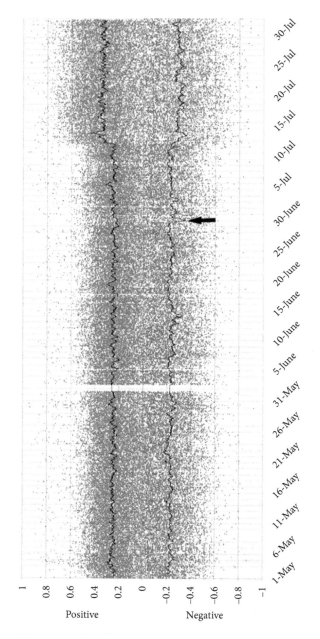

FIGURE 4.4   *Sentiment-classification scatter graph*
Source: Authors' own compilation, derived from collected data.

DOI: 10.1057/9781137496195.0009

to represent visually any interesting movements or trends in the data. As only a short three-month cross-section of data was selected it was not unexpected that there was no clear negative or positive trend in the data. Future studies could, therefore, look at a longer period to determine whether there is a negative or a positive trend in sentiment about democracy on Twitter.

There are a number of anomalies in Figure 4.4 that merit discussion, such as, for example, the gaps in the data. Gaps exist between 11:52 on 31 May and 14:44 on 1 June; also between 02:51 and 04:54 on 15 June; and between 23:52 on 30 June and 02:49 on 1 July. Another big variation in the figure, not explained by the data, is the outward shift that the sentiment makes around 11 July. These gaps and variations were created when the data processing platform updated its beta programme.

On certain days, such as 28 June (indicated by the arrow) there were peaks in the 250 point negative moving average line. After further analysis, some of these peaks tended to indicate Tweets that had been re-Tweeted by many users on a specific day. On 28 June there were two such Tweets that explained the spike in the data. One read as follows:

> **MALAYSIA** @MALAYSIA 🔁
> US has a false democracy, says Mahathir: He says in America they torture people from around the world and that ... http://bit.ly/N5iTqX
> 8:51 AM – 28 Jun 2012

This Tweet related to a Malaysian news story on how Malaysian democracy is truer than American democracy. It was re-Tweeted 32 times within the sample collected for this study.

The next Tweet read:

> **RH Reality Check** @rhrealitycheck 🔁
> RT @MSignorile: Breaking: Conservatives plan 2 leave U.S., but can't find wealthy Western democracy w/ouniversal health care. #hrc #scotus
> 7:43 PM – 28 Jun 2012

This was a re-Tweet of the original Tweet by Mike Signorile, the editor-at-large for the 'Gay Voices Vertical' of *The Huffington Post*, which commented on the US Supreme Court's decision to uphold the Patient Protection and Affordable Care Act (PPACA), colloquially known as 'Obama Care', and how this will affect conservatives in America. It was re-Tweeted 174 times within the sample collected for this study.

Another informative way of representing the sentiment data of the total 104,037 Tweets on the days on which a large number of the same

DOI: 10.1057/9781137496195.0009

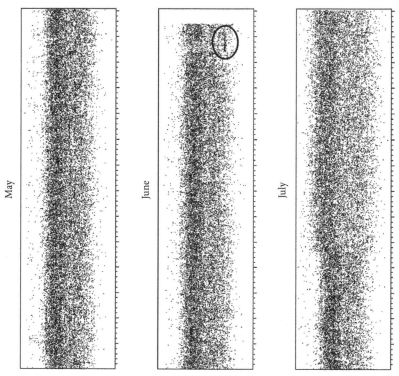

FIGURE 4.5   *Sentiment-classification monthly scatter graphs*
Source: Authors' own compilation, **derived from collected data.**

Tweet was re-Tweeted can be more clearly seen on the next three scatter graphs (Figure 4.5). The dots on these three graphs represent all the Tweets that occurred during each month. It is clearly seen that some of the dots form straight lines. These lines represent the same Tweet that has been re-Tweeted many times over a specific period. One can, for example, see the Signorile Tweet towards the end of the June chart (circled area). Within the Tweet data set, these Tweets were 'trending' and were therefore quite topical. 'Trending' is a term used on various online sites to indicate a topic that is receiving high levels of attention at a specific time. (An example of Twitter trends can be seen on the real time Twitter Trends Map at http://trendsmap.com/.)

The representation of the results in Figure 4.6 answer the descriptive question of whether the majority of the collected Tweets were positive or negative. To do this, the small variance between the classified sentiments

DOI: 10.1057/9781137496195.0009

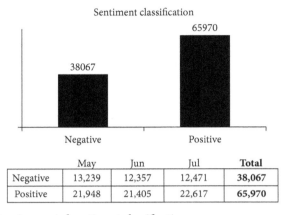

Sentiment classification

	May	Jun	Jul	**Total**
Negative	13,239	12,357	12,471	**38,067**
Positive	21,948	21,405	22,617	**65,970**

FIGURE 4.6   *Aggregated sentiment classification*
Source: Authors' own compilation, derived from collected data.

was not important. In other words, to show whether overall sentiment on expressions of democracy on Twitter is positive or negative for the chosen period each Tweet has only been represented as positive or negative. Any Tweet classified between –1 and 0 will therefore be seen as negative and any Tweet classified between 0 and +1 as positive. In the data collected from the platform this broad positive or negative label has already been added. The results shown in Figure 4.6 were aggregated by counting the entire set of positive and negative Tweets. They showed that the data processing platform classified about 36.6 per cent (30,867) of the collected Tweets as negative and 63.4 per cent (65,970) of the Tweets as positive.

Looking at the Figure 4.6, it would again seem that public expression on democracy, as shown by the sentiment data, is more positive. In fact, the classification showed that in the chosen period there were 27,903 more positive Tweets about democracy than negative.

The relevance and the significance of these findings are twofold. Firstly, it illustrates the possibility and practicality of measuring public expressions on democracy from Twitter using automated computerised methods for the chosen timeframe. Secondly, this method was uncomplicated as it did not require programming skills. It allowed the examination of a constant (except for small gaps in the data) flow of Tweets on democracy that represented 1 per cent of all the Tweets from more than 500 million users on Twitter. As stated earlier, it should be noted

DOI: 10.1057/9781137496195.0009

that this study does not aim to extrapolate to all 500 million users and thus the analysed data are only statistically relevant to the total 104,037 Tweets.

Another consideration of some concern was that the selected commercial data processing platform was still in its development stages, and we were duly cautious about the validity of these results. Further concerns regarding the strange shape of the density graphs in Figures 4.2 and 4.3 prompted a closer examination of the validity of the sentiment classification. The next section contains this analysis.

Measurement validity of the instrument

Although the measurement instrument, namely, the commercial data processing platform, is broadly treated as a 'black box' in this study, it was considered necessary to examine the accuracy and reliability of the instrument more closely by manually testing the validity of the platform.

A random sample of Tweets was collected using a simple random sampling method on the negative and the positive Tweets separately. The two samples, stratified into positive and negative classified Tweets, were then manually classified. In order to achieve a statistical confidence level of 95 per cent and a confidence interval of four, a random sample of 595 Tweets from the positive population of 65,970 was collected and classified. Then to achieve the same level of statistical confidence, a random sample of 591 Tweets of the negative population was also used (see examples of this manual classification in Table 4.2).[13]

Each Tweet in the random sample was examined and then classified as a positive, negative or neutral expression on democracy and assigned a corresponding value +1 for positive, 0 for neutral and –1 for negative. The neutral category was added as many of the Tweets did not contain opinionated data.

There are computerised methods of extracting opinionated key phrases from text and an example of such a method is used by Kumar and Suresha.[14] Certainly, the incorporation of such methods would enable future researchers to extract opinionated Tweets more accurately, but our selected data processing platform, at the stage this research was conducted, did not include this function. For the purpose of this study, it was considered that the incorporation of the neutral classification

DOI: 10.1057/9781137496195.0009

of Tweets would limit the statistical validity of conclusions that can be drawn from the results. The aim was to measure the validity of the measurement instrument, and the most insightful way of doing this was by adding a category for neutral Tweets that did not represent opinions on democracy.

Firstly, the 591 randomly selected Tweets from the 38,067 population of negative Tweets were examined. The negative sample showed that 64 per cent (378) of the Tweets classified as negative by the platform were also negative according to the researchers' subjective opinion. However 7 per cent (43) of the Tweets were wrongly classified – which means that they were actually positive according to us, although the platform had classified them as negative. Lastly, 29 per cent (170) of the random sample of Tweets did not contain opinionated data and were therefore manually classified as neutral. Figure 4.7 illustrates these results in the form of a pie chart.

What these results show is that there is a 95 per cent probability that all of the 38,067 negative Tweets in the population are classified correctly between 59 and 68 per cent of the time (due to the confidence-level and -interval). It is, however, important to note that this percentage is quite high in comparison to manual classification standards. The seminal study by Gale et al.,[15] 'Estimating Upper and Lower Bounds on the Performance of Word-Sense Disambiguation Programs', has shown that when humans classify sentiment statements they tend to agree on only

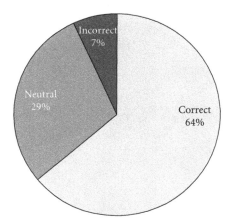

FIGURE 4.7   *Manual classification of negative classified Tweets*
Source: Authors' own compilation, derived from collected data.

DOI: 10.1057/9781137496195.0009

about 68 per cent of the cases. As stated, we agree with the data process-ing platform between 59 and 68 per cent of the time, which means that the programme is between 87 and 100 per cent as accurate as by using manual classification methods to assess the negative Tweets in this study (with a 95% confidence level).

The 595 Tweets from the 65,970 population of positive Tweets were also examined. As expected, when looking at Figures 4.2 and 4.3, the positive sample is not classified nearly as effectively as the negative one. The results show that only 35 per cent (209) of the Tweets classified as positive by the platform were also positive according to the manual judgement. This means that 30 per cent (180) were wrongly classified, or that they were actually negative. About 35 per cent (206) of the Tweets classified as positive by the platform did not contain opinionated data and were therefore manually classified as neutral. Figure 4.8 illustrates these manual results.

What the results in Figure 4.8 show is that there is a 95 per cent chance that all the 65,970 positive Tweets in the population are classified correctly 31–39 per cent of the time. As explained in the table, human sentiment classification correlates on average 68 per cent with each other. The clas-sification performed by the data processing platform was, therefore, only between 46 and 57 per cent accurate when compared with the manual classification of positive Tweets (with a 95% confidence level).

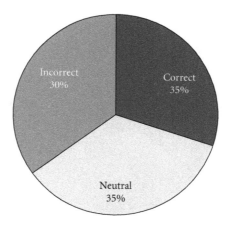

FIGURE 4.8   *Manual classification of positive classified Tweets*
Source: Authors' own compilation, derived from collected data.

DOI: 10.1057/9781137496195.0009

Discussion of results

The selected commercial data processing platform, therefore, performed well with classifying negative Tweets regarding democracy, but less well with classifying positive Tweets. There were also quite large segments of each selection that were neutral Tweets without any sentiments on democracy in general or about a specific country.

With this new information it was possible to estimate more closely the actual amount of positive and negative Tweets contained within the total population of collected Tweets. It is imperative to note that this is, however, still a subjective estimation and will only represent a range of possibility that the Tweets would have been classified as positive or negative manually. To limit this subjectivity, future research could increase the number of participants that classify the Tweet sample and, as mentioned, other measuring platforms can also be used. Furthermore, the results are only indicative of the 104,037 collected Tweets and contain limitations to the validity, expressed earlier, due to the added neutral category.

Figure 4.9 represents the new estimation on the proportion of the Tweets that were classified as either positive or negative from the data calculated in the previous table. From this figure one can see that, according to our subjective estimations, the approximate amount of

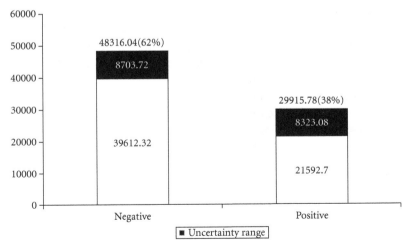

FIGURE 4.9   *Estimation of approximate sentiment levels*
Source: Authors' own compilation.

DOI: 10.1057/9781137496195.0009

negative Tweets for the given period were between 39,612 and 48,316. The approximate amount of positive Tweets was estimated to be between 21,593 and 29,916.

Error range in platform classification

These results showed that the platform sentiment classification, when performed on the selected Tweets about democracy, were less than accurate. In fact, there was a variance of 3.9–21 per cent in the negative classification when the results were compared to the manual results. The positive classification, in turn, showed a variance of 55–67 per cent when comparing the platform results to the manual results. The calculations for this variance are as follows:

Negative variance:

$$100 - (38067/39612.32*100) = 3.90110955379538$$
$$100 - (38067/48316.04*100) = 21.21250003104559$$

Positive variance:

$$100 - (21592.7/65970*100) = 67.26891011065636$$
$$100 - (29915.78/65970*100) = 54.65244808246173$$

However, it should be noted that this platform was still in its beta testing stages when this research was conducted and, therefore, the larger error range is understandable. Furthermore, the platform has neither been created specifically for measuring sentiment on democracy nor 'trained' (i.e., a method of teaching/training the programme with large sets of data in order to make analysis more accurate) specifically for analysing data on democracy. More advanced sentiment analysis software, especially software that has been specifically trained to examine political data, would vastly improve the results of this study. Another recommendation for future researchers, who would like to conduct this type of study on a larger scale, would be to get access to the full Twitter stream. This would allow them to make more direct conclusions about the full population of Twitter users than found in this study.

Feasibility of measuring public expressions on democracy via Twitter

It was found that it is possible to measure public expressions on democracy from interest- articulated sentiments gathered from a sample of

DOI: 10.1057/9781137496195.0009

Tweets processed with content analysis and sentiment analysis software. The method of using this platform to gather and analyse Tweets for the chosen period was therefore successful.

It has been shown that the automated classification of negative Tweets was almost as effective as using human judgement. However, automated method was much faster than manual classification as these results are calculated almost instantly by the platform. Nevertheless, there are concerns with the level of accuracy obtained in the classification of the positive Tweets as the platform seems to have had problems with classifying positive sentiments relating to democracy in the collected Tweets.

This means that the level of accuracy is limited if one views this platform as the current level of technology for automated sentiment analysis of Tweets relating to democracy. However, as this platform is still in its infancy these methods are being improved constantly. There are also other platforms and programmes that could be used in future studies. Nevertheless, despite problems with the accuracy of the measurement instrument, it is possible to measure public expressions on democracy with the aforementioned methods.

The closest quantitative description that this study can give for this limitation of accuracy and extent, as expressed in the chapter, is that the results show that a variance of 3.9–21 per cent exists in the negative classification when the results are compared to the manual results. The positive classification, in turn, shows a variance of 55–67 per cent when the results are compared to the manual results.

What this means is that, by using the data processing platform to measure negative public expressions on democracy, in 79–96.1 per cent of cases it gives the same results compared to our manual reading through a sample of all 104,037 Tweets. For the positive public expression classifications, the study finds that the platform will produce the same results between 33 and 45 per cent of cases. The extent of the method developed in this study is, therefore, limited to the level of technology that is available and as these methods improve, the extent will also improve.

We do, however, believe that even if the extent of measured public expressions on democracy is limited, it can still be a helpful tool in supplementing survey data. For example, the relatively high level of accuracy in measuring negative sentiment on democracy from the Tweet data can give insights as to what the main issues are with democracy within a specific section of the population. This is discussed in more detail in the section to follow on future research.

DOI: 10.1057/9781137496195.0009

Other findings

Apart from answering the research questions, this study also found a number of other interesting findings. Firstly, as shown here, one is able to see the effect of certain real-world events on the collected Tweet data. It has been shown how certain Tweets are re-Tweeted and become trending topics that can be clearly seen on a scatter graph of Tweet sentiment (Figures 4.4 and 4.5). These trending Tweets might be a good starting point for future researchers to examine topical issues within a set of Tweets.

Secondly, it is interesting to note that there is no apparent trend when one views the sentiment data for democracy Tweets over the period of three months. Prior to this study, it was believed by these researchers that a trend would emerge even if such a short cross-section was chosen. If future researchers are to look for a trend in the sentiment data, it is recommended that a longer period is chosen.

Thirdly, a number of anomalies in the data emerge when the data are plotted on a scatter graph. There are clearly gaps in the data and outward shifts in the classification of sentiment. This led the researchers to contact the platform to confirm whether these were changes in the platform and not in the data. Although these anomalies affect this introductory study minimally, it is certainly something that future studies might look out for if using a platform such as this one.

Fourthly, as seen from the literature on the development of democracy the apparent 'evolution' of democracy seems to be strongly influenced by public opinion. This opinion, according to Habermas,[16] is, to an extent, created in the public sphere. If one views Twitter as part of the public sphere, as done in this study, it becomes possible for the functioning of democracy to be affected by what people are saying on Twitter. Even though it was known that people were talking about democracy and that some of these opinions were negative, it is fascinating to see the complexity of some of the expressions and dialogue about democracy on Twitter. It is also interesting to see how much information one could gather from these Tweets.

One example is the Tweet by Michelangelo Signorile on 28 June which was re-Tweeted more than 174 times within the collected data. Here is an example of a re-Tweet of this original Tweet by RH Reality Check:

RH Reality Check @rhrealitycheck
RT @MSignorile: Breaking: Conservatives plan 2 leave U.S., but can't find wealthy Western democracy w/ouniversal health care. #hrc #scotus
7:43 PM – 28 Jun 2012

DOI: 10.1057/9781137496195.0009

Fifthly, RH Reality Check by their own definition 'is an online community and publication serving individuals and organizations committed to advancing sexual and reproductive health and rights'.[17] They have more than 12,000 followers which means that this re-Tweet was potentially seen on 12,000 accounts. On 28 June, @rhrealitycheck tweeted another 49 times about the US federal court ruling on the PPACA. All of this information and other potential information, such as the location of the person tweeting, can be gained from looking at the Tweet data.

The sixth additional finding of this study relates to the colloquial versions of the term 'democracy' used in the Tweet data. After the analysis of the Tweet data, it was found that the words 'demockerycy, democratees, democrabeep, democrackcy, democrack, democrapsy, democrass D3mocr@cy and demo-crazy' were not used in any of the collected Tweets. Also, it should be noted that as the platform does not look at capital letters (upper case), searching for both 'Democracy' and 'democracy' is redundant. In addition, it is also redundant to search for both terms such as 'democracy' and 'liberal democracy', as the platform would find all versions of 'democracy', including 'liberal democracy' from the keyword 'democracy'.

The study also observes that, similar to news media, where negative news receives priority and more coverage,[18] Twitter also contains more negative than positive expressions. The ramifications of this observation are, however, not tested in this study and we are unaware of any studies that have explicitly shown that people speak more negatively on Twitter. However, if this is the case, it might partly explain why the final estimations of expressions on democracy in this study show an expression of more negative than positive sentiments and this could guide future studies.

Deeper questions such as whether democracy actually offers an optimal political system of governance lie at the background to this study about creating instruments to measure expressions on democracy. We, like most democrats, agree with Churchill's well-known statement that '[d]emocracy is the worst form of government, except for all those other forms that have been tried from time to time'. The concomitant belief is that citizens are better able to decide on their own interests than any other agents, be it dictators, experts, military rulers, one-party regimes and/or hereditary monarchs who would do so on behalf of citizens. This in turn pre-supposes certain levels of competence from citizens, as is claimed to be present in the Civic Culture, and, especially, about the cognitive capabilities of humans and its effect on democracy.

DOI: 10.1057/9781137496195.0009

An enlightening study about the mental aptitude of people was conducted by David Dunning and Justin Kruger and published in 1999. According to their study, people generally hold overly favourable views of their own abilities – which impact their interaction in many social and intellectual domains. The exception is that those participants with higher metacognitive competence recognised their limitations and therefore scored their abilities lower than those with a lower metacognitive competence.[19] This cognitive bias that people hold towards their own capabilities is popularly called the Dunning-Kruger effect. Could this effect be registered in the millions of Tweets being sent out daily: smarter Twitter users may be more reticent in railing against democracy, while less smart Twitter users do so with far less inhibitions?

In addition, one can, for example, look at The Twitter Political Index. This is a website created by Twitter to show the percentage of positive sentiment Tweets that were being tweeted regarding the 2012 US presidential candidates, Barack Obama and Mitt Romney. The results on this website indicated that both Obama and Romney, on average, scored well below 50 per cent. What this means is that Tweets concerning both candidates were more negative than positive. For example, on 17 September 2012 Obama only received 20 per cent positive Tweets and Romney only 9 per cent.[20] Yet, if one compares Twitter's positive sentiment data to the much higher approval rating on traditional opinion polls (around 50% for both candidates)[21] it might indicate that people express more negative sentiment on Twitter than they do in traditional opinion polls. However, as Twitter users are a specific section of the population that Tweet about political candidates, it is perhaps not an accurate measurement to compare with an opinion poll based on the entire population. As such, future studies on determining the general level of negative sentiment on social media sites such as Twitter is warranted. These types of studies might show if sentiment on this form of media in general is more negative and, if so, why this is the case. It could also support the results of this study as it would give a better understanding on sentiment statements collected from Twitter.

Future research

As stated throughout this book, this is an introductory study to develop and test the methodology of measuring public expressions on democracy

DOI: 10.1057/9781137496195.0009

from Twitter. The aim, therefore, is to open up the field for future research for measuring public expressions from social media sites. Owing to the introductory nature of this research, it is impossible to look at all the potential uses of measuring public expressions from social media sites. In this section, therefore, further potential analyses using variations of this study are examined. The goal is to provide insights that might be of benefit to future studies.

Firstly, this study focused on the topic of democracy, but this could be replicated with any topic of a researcher's choosing. If people are discussing a topic on the Internet, and specifically Twitter for this study, the methodology described in this study could be used to extract and analyse expressions on that topic.

Secondly, Twitter was chosen as the online social media network for this study as Tweets are relatively freely available in the public sphere and a large section of the global population is represented by these Tweets. Furthermore, the Tweets are short which makes it easier to analyse than, say, looking at full blogs. It would, however, be possible to extract information from other social media sites such as Facebook, and look at blogs and even extract information from mobile social networks such as WhatsApp – if one can gain access to the data. It should be noted that companies such as DataSift, for example, can provide access to a much larger range of social media sites, but this option is quite costly. The automated sentiment analysis method used in this study is, however, only limited to textual data at present.

There are a number of ways in which a future researcher can get an even deeper understanding of collected data. This study focusses only on the sentiment as classified by this platform and the researchers' subjective analysis. Tweets, however, contain much more than just sentiment. For example, one could look at the location identification tags that are attached to some of the Tweets. This would make it possible for future research to examine expressions from a specific area of the world. It should, however, be stated that at present a user has to activate a location setting personally for it to be seen in the public realm.

The Tweet data, of course, also contains quite a lot of other information that can be extracted with further quantitative or qualitative methods. On the quantitative side, for example, one might count the number of words used in all the Tweets with a simple programme. As an illustration, we have extracted some of the most used terms and some interesting words relating to the term 'democracy' and automatically counted

DOI: 10.1057/9781137496195.0009

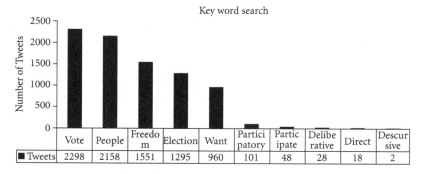

FIGURE 4.10   *Key word search*
Source: Authors' own compilation.

the number of times that it was mentioned in the collected Tweets. With this method, as shown in Figure 4.10, one can see what central concepts are being discussed in connection with the chosen topic.

The suggestion is that the most common themes can then be used to guide a qualitative analysis about what is being said within the Tweets themselves. A useful aid in this task is an automated topic extraction programme. These programmes have been discussed in studies by both Chang et al.[22] and Tiun et al.,[23] which attempt to extract the most relevant topics from a set of data. Our study, in turn, attempted to manually extract a rough topic cluster subjectively, examples of which can be found in Table 4.2.

It can be seen that we looked at the most common themes that we believe are relevant to the topic of democracy. From the collected Tweet data it appears that a lot of Tweets reflect on how democracy is being devalued by corporate interests and money politics. The following is an example of this type of Tweet:

> **sunshineejc** @sunshineejc
> Why do Americans Allow corporations to co-opt our democracy by granting them the rights of legal personhood and defining money as speech #p2
> 3:43 AM – 10 Jul 2012

Another theme extracted was to do with problems about the functioning of democracy as seen in Tweets such as:

> **Diane Ravitch** @DianeRavitch
> When we lose neighborhood schools, we lose community. We lose a building block of democracy where people learn to take action. #soschat
> 4:45 AM – 20 Jun 2012

DOI: 10.1057/9781137496195.0009

TABLE 4.2   *Negative sentiment groups*

4.2.1   Financial corruption and democracy

Suzan Hayden @AstroSHayden 📩
Mitt Romney and the whole GOP party is dangerous for America. When Koch
    Brothers can destroy democracy by buying GOP, DANGEROUS
8:31 AM – 9 May 2012

Tim Lezard @TolpuddleTim 📩
Today's market news: rich people worried that poor people might take some of their
    wealth off them as democracy intervenes in profit-making
10:44 AM – 7 May 2012

Dr. Jill Stein @DrJillStein 📩
'We don't need to run America like a business or like the military. We need to run
    America like a democracy.' PLS RT
4:01 PM – 27 Jun 2012

Mick Gill @Mick_Gill 📩
Think Democracy only benefits the Rich and oppresses the Poor. Shameful amount of
    Poor in a Country like US for example.
6:50 PM – 2 Jun 2012

Yuri Klastalov @klastalov 📩
Democracy is a form of government that substitutes election by the incompetent many
    for appointment by the corrupt few. – G.B. Shaw
7:46 PM – 29 Jun 2012

4.2.2   The functioning of democracy

Foreign Affairs @ForeignAffairs 📩
Bad judges! #Pakistan's supreme court is undermining democracy: http://fam.ag/
    OtPIDb
4:48 PM – 5 Jul 2012

Diane Ravitch @DianeRavitch 📩
When we lose neighborhood schools, we lose community. We lose a building block of
    democracy where people learn to take action. #soschat
4:45 AM – 20 Jun 2012

generationOn @generationOn 📩
The Moment of #Youth. Our Kids are Failing #Democracy. @DrPriceMitchell
    describes how to can engage youth in #service. http://bit.ly/MycQk3
7:40 PM – 30 Jun 2012

Glenn Greenwald @ggreenwald 📩
I wonder what percentage of Americans know their government is constantly bombing
    Yemen & killing civilians? #Democracy
5:21 PM – 15 May 2012

WhiteHousePressCorps @whpresscorps 📩
RT @politicalmath: Man ... I wish my vote counted as 'democracy.' Apparently only D
    votes count.
5:56 AM – 6 Jun 2012

DOI: 10.1057/9781137496195.0009

TABLE 4.2   *Continued*

4.2.3   Pure negative expressions on democracy

Wayolwa Kombwa @ChantingWarrior 🔄
My friend Kasweka is right. This eviction and destroying of people's Kambashus is
   oppression. Theres no sign of democracy here ... eeee
4:48 PM – 14 Jun 2012

مقاومة @IntifadaDude 🔄
Iraq Veteran: 'I'm returning my medals because under the guise of democracy I stole
   Iraq's humanity and lost mine.' #NoNato @OccupyChicago
12:18 AM – 21 May 2012

Shofwan Al Banna @ShofwanAlBanna 🔄
Another forgotten massacre: Kashmir. Within a so-called democracy http://www.
   nytimes.com/2012/07/08/opinion/sunday/indias-blood-stained-democracy.
   html ... 12:52 PM – 7 Jul 2012

Anonymous @YourAnonNews 🔄
Error 404 Democracy Not Found - #ACTA vs #OpTequila
5:32 PM – 12 Jul 2012

Brian Leskovec @bisonranchr68 🔄
#IAmARepublicanBecause I love Democracy so much that I'm working hard to allow
   FASCISM to overthrow it
2:43 PM – 14 Jun 2012

Source: Twitter, 2012.

Lastly, a topic was extracted that contains Tweets which are simply
blatant negative sentences regarding democracy, such as:

> Anonymous @YourAnonNews 🔄
> Error 404 Democracy Not Found - #ACTA vs #OpTequila
> 5:32 PM – 12 Jul 2012

Using this type of qualitative analysis it might be possible to extract the
issues that are most prominent with regard to the specific topic, in this
case 'democracy'.

Future studies might also benefit from including more advanced
data collection and analysis methods. The use of NLP methods would
ensure that the sentiment analysis software can more accurately analyse
the collected data. The NLP software would convert the Tweet data into
natural language that is more easily understandable to the sentiment
analysis software. The NLP technique harnesses the computational
capabilities of computers, which analyse naturally occurring texts and
then process these texts (using one or more levels of linguistic analysis)
to produce usable and congruent (correct) text. In future studies NLP
could be used to turn Tweets such as:

DOI: 10.1057/9781137496195.0009

> Wn We Spk of 'Democracy' in Wch Rt.2 Vote is included then Obviously RT.2 REJECT shud b CONSTRUED As A Concurrent Right !!! (illustrative example only, compiled by authors)

Into this:

> When we speak of democracy, in which the right to vote is included, then obviously the right to reject should be construed as a concurrent right!

This would allow the sentiment classification software to classify the Tweets more accurately in terms of a better understanding of the sentence.

Finally, more advanced sentiment analysis software, especially software that has been specifically trained to examine political data, would vastly improve the results of a study such as this. Furthermore, researchers with advanced programming knowledge could consider the automated non-parametric content analysis method designed specifically for the social sciences by Hopkins and King.[24]

Conclusion

The data presentation of this chapter shows that Twitter can at best be described as an incipient public sphere. As is shown in this chapter, even very generalised, rudimentary sentiments, such as positive or negative orientations to democracy, are expressed in as many distinct ways as there are individuals who Tweet. As reviewed in Chapter 3, the Habermasian conception of the public sphere holds that such expressions become part of and constitute the public sphere if and when they 'coalesce into bundles of topically specified public opinions'.[25] For this process of coalescence to occur, this mass of individual self-expressed opinion needs to be merged into categories of expressions in some way similar to one another. The sentiment analysis demonstrated in this chapter is a first step in such a process. This results in the re-arranging of the mass of individual Tweets into a (again, very basic) more structured arrangement of expressions. For these expressions to gain the impact that public opinion holds in established democracies another step is required: individual tweeters should be able to identify themselves, through a process of reflection as being located within any one of such categories, or, as still being outside of any and every such constructed category. From such a process of self-identification it becomes possible for individuals to imagine themselves

DOI: 10.1057/9781137496195.0009

as being of a like mind to others who do so too, and from that conviction a new community, and a new sense of community, can emerge. This is the topic of the next chapter.

Notes

1   As mentioned in Chapter 1, this commercial firm allowed us to use the results of the research undertaken by them, but declined to be named.

2   B. O'Connor et al. (2010) *From Tweets to Polls: Linking Text Sentiment to Public Opinion Time Series*, in Proceedings of ICWSM: Carnegie Mellon University.

3   D.J. Hopkins and G. King (2010) 'A Method of Automated Nonparametric Content Analysis for Social Science', *American Journal of Political Science*, 54(1), 229–247.

4   J. Yi et al. (2003) *Sentiment Analyzer: Extracting Sentiments about a Given Topic Using Natural Language Processing Techniques*. IEEE International Conference on Data Mining (ICDM), 427–434.

5   Yi et al., *Sentiment Analyzer*; B. Pang, B. Lee and S. Vaithyanathan (2002) *Thumbs Up? Sentiment Classification Using Machine Learning Technique*, Proceedings of EMNLP, 79–86.

6   O'Connor et al., *From Tweets to Polls*.

7   Note that it is unnecessary to add capital letters as the programme searches for these automatically. It is also unnecessary to search for the terms 'democracy' and 'liberal democracy' as the search for 'democracy' will include phrases on liberal democracy.

8   'Noisy' in this case refers to the difficulty of computers to understand, analyse and interpret the data.

9   O'Connor et al., *From Tweets to Polls*.

10 Twitter Developers (2012) *The Streaming APIs* (Online, available at: https://dev.twitter.com/docs/streaming-apis [31/07/2012]).

11 Twitter Developers, *The Streaming APIs*.

12 DataSift (2012) *Unlock Trends from Public Tweets* (Online, available at: http://datasift.com/historics/ [31/07/2012]).

13 The required sample size was calculated with Creative Research System's Sample Size Calculator (http://www.surveysystem.com/sscalc.htm). The full classification is also available and can be provided if needed (email bflutz@gmail.com).

14 A.K.M. Kumar and A. Suresha (2010) 'An Empirical Approach for Opinion Detection Using Significant Sentences', *International Journal of Advanced Engineering & Application*, 6335, 486–497.

15 W. Gale, K.W. Church and D. Yarowsky (1992) *Estimating Upper and Lower Bounds on the Performance of Word-Sense Disambiguation Programs*, in

Proceedings of the 30th Annual Meeting on Association for Computational Linguistics (ACL '92). Association for Computational Linguistics, Stroudsburg, PA, USA, 249–256.

16   J. Habermas (1989) *The Structural Transformation of the Public Sphere: An Inquiry into a Category of Bourgeois Society* (Cambridge: Polity Press).

17   RHRealityCheck (2012) About Us. *RH Reality Check* (Online, available at: http://www.rhrealitycheck.org/about-us [09/13/2012]).

18   W. Gieber (1955) 'Do Newspapers Overplay "Negative" News?', *Journalism & Mass Communication Quarterly*, 32, 311–318.

19   J. Kruger and D. Dunning (1999) 'Unskilled and Unaware of It: How Difficulties in Recognizing One's Own Incompetence Lead to Inflated Self-Assessments', *Journal of Personality and Social Psychology*, 77(6), 1121–1134.

20   Elections.Twitter (2012) *The Twitter Political Index* (Online, available at: https://election.twitter.com/ [18/09/2012]).

21   Real Clear Politics (2012) *General Election: Romney vs. Obama* (Online, available at: http://www.realclearpolitics.com/epolls/2012/president/us/general_election_romney_vs_obama-1171.html [18/09/2012]); J. Zeleny (2012) 'Poll: Obama Holds Narrow Edge over Romney', *The New York Times* (Online, available at: http://thecaucus.blogs.nytimes.com/2012/09/14/poll-obama-holds-narrow-edge-over-romney/ [18/09/2012]); CNN (2012) *CNN ORC Poll* (Online, available at: http://i2.cdn.turner.com/cnn/2012/images/09/10/rel10a.pdf [18/09/2012]).

22   J. Chang et al. (2002) *Topic Extraction from Text Documents Using Multiple-Cause Networks*, School of Computer Science and Engineering, Seoul National University.

23   S. Tiun, R. Abdullah and T.E. Kong (2001) 'Automatic Topic Identification Using Ontology Hierarchy', *Computational Linguistics and Intelligent Text Processing* 2004/2001, 444–453.

24   Hopkins and King, 'A Method of Automated Nonparametric Content Analysis for Social Science', 229–247.

25   J. Habermas (1996) *Between Facts and Norms* (Cambridge, MA: MIT Press), p. 360.

DOI: 10.1057/9781137496195.0009

5
New Imagined Communities in the Digital Age

Abstract: *In this chapter we return to the theme of democracy and its social base. Current impacts are dramatically demonstrated in the social movements of the Arab Spring, with Tunisia and Egypt as the leading examples. The brief surge of the Occupy Wall Street movement, replicated in many cities throughout the world, is also notable, both for its global manifestation and for its fleeting existence. This section is closed by outlining what we consider to be the conditions for the creation of new imagined communities and of the contribution the data analysis method we developed hold in this field. We conclude that social media holds huge promise for democracy in the capacity of interest articulation but falls short with interest aggregation. We consider this process as one of the key steps to attain effective interest aggregation, which in turn is conducive to regaining social cohesion and the formation of new imagined communities.*

Keywords: Arab Spring; coalescence; new imagined communities; Occupy Wall Street; self-reflection; social movements; totalitarian societies

Lutz, Barend and Pierre du Toit. *Defining Democracy in a Digital Age: Political Support on Social Media.* Basingstoke: Palgrave Macmillan, 2014. DOI: 10.1057/9781137496195.0010.

The Internet-based communications revolution is a technological work-in-progress as are the changes in the social base of democracy being made by these forces. Some aspects of the current impact of Internet-based social media, however, are already apparent and can be described with the concepts of democratic theory. This chapter examines a selection of studies of both the current and prospective future impact of Internet-based technology to construct a conceptual framework within which to appraise the data analysis methodology used in the sentiment analysis demonstrated in the previous chapter. This appraisal serves as an answer to the primary question about the construction of new, imagined communities with which to buttress democracy in the Digital Age. Our answer, in a nutshell, is that the methodology of quantitative sentiment analysis can serve two purposes. The first is as an instrument to measure support for democracy within that part of the public sphere created by the digital social media. The second is as a mechanism which can aid individuals to imagine themselves as being part of new, more stable, more enduring and potentially more effective communities that are able to re-construct a social base for democracies in the new Digital Age.

The Internet: current impact

An early indication of the impact of the Internet in conventional democratic politics was revealed in the role social media played in political interest articulation and mobilisation in Barack Obama's victory in the 2008 American presidential election.

The leading examples of such social media are Twitter, Facebook and YouTube, which involve mass personal communication from within the private sphere where individuals have full control over the content of what they release on these media. Each entry is uniquely individualised and can be fully autonomous from entries by other actors. Its potential reach is as far as the Internet penetrates and connects the global population, which makes for global amplification. By 2010, the Internet connected more than two billion people, and by 2025 most of the world's population, projected to be then about eight billion, is likely to be connected to the web.[1] Given this potential, social media has a huge latent capacity to facilitate the growth of bridging social capital.

DOI: 10.1057/9781137496195.0010

The politics of revolt

The impact of these media on the politics of interest articulation outside of the channels of conventional democratic politics was also powerfully demonstrated in the early events of the so-called Arab Spring, which started in January 2011 with the revolt against the 23-year-old dictatorship of President Zine al-Abidine Ben Ali of Tunisia. The decisive trigger for the revolt occurred on 17 December 2010 in the town of Sidi Bouzid when Mohamed Bouazizi, a local fruit vendor, set himself alight – with lethal consequences for himself – in protest against the humiliating harassment he received from the local police. He died of his wounds on 4 January 2011, but the incident itself rapidly initiated street protests in the town where police then killed a number of youthful demonstrators.

The incident and its consequences rapidly became an international news event due to many of these protests being recorded on cellphone videos, which were then posted on the Internet – especially on Facebook. The television news network *Al Jazeera* picked up on the story from there, and as the protests gained momentum, more violent repression by the state became video material for yet more Internet postings. Another consideration is that the Internet's amplification of these events in Tunisia itself was made possible by the deep penetration of the Internet in Tunisian society. At the time, one in three Tunisians was an Internet user, and 91 per cent of Tunisian students visited Facebook daily. According to survey data, 64 per cent of these students said Facebook was their primary source of information about the protests.[2] Of particular relevance was that the Internet users on Facebook in Tunisia far exceeded that of the other Arab states of Morocco, Egypt, Algeria, Libya and Yemen.[3]

On 14 January 2011 the decisive moment occurred with a mass protest in the capital Tunis. The regular army under General Rachid Ammar took and held the city centre. Ammar first refused Ben Ali's instruction to use sharp ammunition against the protesters: instead he arrested the head of the Presidential Guard, who apparently was planning a *coup d'état*. The army then took further initiatives in steering the transition. When Ben Ali resigned it was the army that secured the airport, which then allowed him to flee the country. Thereafter, they acted to prevent the Presidential Guard from instigating terror attacks against the civilian population. The final tipping point for regime change came on 27 February 2011 when all the remaining ministers in Ben Ali's government resigned.

DOI: 10.1057/9781137496195.0010

On 25 January 2011, a very similar series of events started to play out in Egypt. This time Tahrir Square in Cairo became centre stage. The main player was again a dictatorial president – Hosni Mubarak. The protests were led by a range of civic organisations, which mobilised mass demonstrations via the Internet-connected public and the army. The sequence of events was also similar: with the help of their web-based networks, the huge public rejection of the Mubarak regime was organised in Tahrir Square. As his authority crumbled, the army took over and removed him from office while it guided the administration towards regime change.[4]

Another fleeting social movement that was facilitated by social media was the Occupy Wall Street campaign, which started in New York in August 2011 and rapidly spread to about 900 cities in 80 countries. Collectively described as 'Occupy... the World' this movement modelled itself on the *Indignados*, who occupied the centre of Madrid for months on end during 2011. Besides their very prominent physical and symbolic presence, the demands of these gatherings were not very clear[5] and at times perceived as incoherent. The movement failed to find clarity on objectives and/or strategies and tactics beyond the city squares where they gathered and disassembled within a few months.

Once demands from citizens are clearly articulated, the next step in achieving citizen effectiveness is to aggregate these demands in a coherent way. Interest aggregation, defined as '[t]he function of converting demands into general policy alternatives',[6] provides structure to the variety of articulated demands and/or to the many ways in which similar demands are expressed. Structure is provided in the sense that demands are categorised, which then makes it possible to rank them in terms of preference. Structure is a necessary condition for coherence.

This, social media has yet to accomplish effectively. As stated previously, one of the early successful recent instances of citizens acting effectively was during the 2008 Obama election campaign when the social networking capacities of social media platforms were used in tandem with the traditional methods of door-to-door campaigning and within the established institutional structures of political parties and electoral machinery. Social media provided the platform for articulating preferences, and the party machines aggregated these into electoral choices.[7] In the case of Tunisia and Egypt, however, it was the military that provided the decisive physical presence to take power at the centre and to provide the institutional framework for making and executing crucial policy decisions. In Egypt, this has happened twice in recent times. In July

DOI: 10.1057/9781137496195.0010

2013, mass gatherings at Tahrir Square once again served as a powerful symbolic rejection of the ruling Muslim Brotherhood under President Mohamed Morsi, but it took the military to follow through by converting this public sentiment into the policy action of arresting Morsi.[8] And, quite tellingly, the military then proceeded to impose their own agenda of transformation onto the Egyptian society. The Muslim Brotherhood was banned, new elections were called and the then minister of defence, Abdel Fattah al-Sisi, retired from his position to contest the election. He duly won the 2014 presidential election held from 26 to 8 May 2014 with 96.91 per cent of the votes, a result that was widely received with scepticism. Another vivid demonstration of this weakness has been with the Occupy...movement. No army, no political party machine or any other institution came to take up the demands of the protesters in any significant way.

The general appraisal of the role of these social media-driven political events made by Eric Schmidt and Jared Cohen in their book *The New Digital Age: Reshaping the Future of People, Nations and Business* is as follows.[9] For a start, they argue, given the huge amount of agency this media allows individual users, followers are likely to join multiple issue-based movements at the same time. Consequently, with such agency this support can be turned off as easily as it is turned on, so the manifestation of demands remains unstable and fickle. This can lead to the repeated creation of new imagined communities of the most ephemeral kind, with the Occupy...movement as a striking example.

Secondly, the institutional vacuum that arises when mobilisation through social media is not dovetailed with established political party machinery will continue, with the resultant lack of policy outcomes. The effect, as Schmidt and Cohen note, is that revolutionary movements may become more easy to generate, but also more difficult to complete. As they put it: 'You cannot storm an interior ministry by mobile phone'.[10]

Thirdly, technology alone does not nurture or select leaders on the ground – it can produce instant celebrities, veritable nine-day-wonders, some of whom may turn out to be false prophets and who raise expectations of revolutionary outcomes, but they do little to construct the capacity of such movements to do so. At times, leaders in such conditions of social upheaval may well be required to go against the momentum of publicly expressed sentiment to oppose the 'mad consensus'[11] created by huge numbers of highly agitated individuals who say exactly what they want to via social media platforms.

DOI: 10.1057/9781137496195.0010

Fourthly, Schmidt and Cohen warn about the internal logic of revolutionary action. When established authoritarian rulers are displaced, a power vacuum necessarily emerges. The deeper this vacuum (in the sense that institutions that maintain social order are dismantled) and the longer it persists, the weaker the prospects for democratic outcomes. They draw on the words of Henry Kissinger, '[T]he more authority is destroyed, the more absolute the authority that follows is (*sic*)'.[12]

Finally, Schmidt and Cohen note that the role of social media in sustaining and extending democracy will continue to be shaped by the censorship and surveillance efforts by governments, both authoritarian[13] and democratic.[14]

New social movements

A strikingly different interpretation of the nature, structure and significance of the Occupy ... movement is presented by Manuel Castells in his book *Networks of Outrage and Hope. Social Movements in the Internet Age.* For a start, he recognises that the lack of formal leadership, one of its most obvious organisational features, is not a matter of neglect, ineptness, laziness or sloth but is rather a deliberate strategic and symbolic organisational objective. The object of the movement is to establish, both in the terrain of cyberspace and of symbolic urban space, a form of direct, deliberative democracy. This organisational form is in itself a statement, and it is (was) driven by the complete breakdown in trust in the established institutions of representative democracy. This leaderless organisational form, according to Castells, expresses the disgust, outrage and alienation of a particular cohort of citizens with contemporary democracies and especially the ties that formal elected representatives have with the formal institutions of global financial capitalism. In the United States, the financial sector that is physically and symbolically represented by the Wall Street address, and the historic links that executives from these firms have had with the federal governments – even in the case of the Obama administration – provided the epitome of what this movement objected to, rejected and revolted against.[15] For the Occupy ... movement to establish a layered hierarchy with a clearly identified leadership would be to commit, yet again, the errors of the very form of organisation they were opposing. Instead, they sought, very deliberately, to establish a consensus-seeking model, in which process would be more important than outcomes.

DOI: 10.1057/9781137496195.0010

The challenge to the existing democratic order was initially at least focussed on global financial capitalism, but its demands rapidly diversified into a multitude of specific grievances, few, if any, expressed as coherent demands for policy action. For some, the object was not even to express demands as such into the political system, but rather to 'assert' themselves and what they stood for in the urban public spaces they occupied. Castells argued that the ultimate long-term goal for social movements was to shape society by inducing a change in values, to affect both popular and political culture towards a new, open, deliberative society, and away from hierarchy, away from entrenched power structures and towards new forms of accountability.[16]

One of these values was that of non-violence, a difficult one to hold onto, as they were intent on openly challenging a very firmly established order. In the assessment of Castells, they did succeed in this, even against the very worst actions of provocateurs.[17] Another value was that of equality. Revolt against the massive social and economic inequality that was building up in the 'new economy' of mature capitalism was a tangible target, vividly expressed in symbolic terms with the depiction of a society divided between the rich 1 per cent and the deprived 99 per cent. The right to assert themselves outside the formal channels of political participation, that is, not through political parties, interest groups and elections but rather through civil disobedience, was another cherished value.

Castells also singles out the values of individuation and autonomy. Individuation is defined as an orientation to action in which the individual is seen as the 'paramount principle orientating his/her behaviour'.[18] This need not be individualism, as the individual could select altruistic objectives to support. Autonomy refers to the capacity of actors, whether individual or collective, to identify and pursue objectives not only independently from the major institutions of society, but more in terms of the values of the particular actor. For Castells, the technology of the Internet makes it possible to achieve both given the freedom of choice available to its users and the capacity for networking that is available through the Internet.[19]

Lastly, and important for this study, Castells notes that the Occupy...movement is highly self-reflective; 'they constantly interrogate themselves as movements, and as individuals, about who they are, what they want to achieve, which kind of democracy and society they wish for'.[20] Their primary Internet forums are blogs and discussion groups on social media. These forums then also serve as sites of information about themselves, so providing the basic material on which they are to reflect.

A number of the mentioned attributes of the Occupy ... movement resonate with that of the counter-culture movement of the 1960s. However, one major difference is the level of technology available to the actors. The 1960s counter-culture faded in the 1970s and most of its members blended into the establishment they so despised. But some of their values (on equality of the sexes, on the civil rights movement, on war and on environmental degradation, to name a few) did seep into the mainstream popular culture of Western democracies to produce some lasting social impact. The immediate question is whether the Occupy ... movement, with a much more powerful communication platform in the shape of the Internet at its disposal will be better off to do the same, or not. Much will depend on what kind of popular culture is being carried by the Internet and more importantly is being shaped by the Internet. We will return to this question at the end of the chapter.

New imagined communities

From the earlier mentioned overview of the impact of the Internet-based social media on democratic politics one can start to identify some of the conditions of the social base conducive to sustaining durable imagined communities in the Digital Age. Firstly, the review of the literature in Chapter 2 shows that a society is required in which individuals are socially engaged in the form of both bonding and bridging social capital so that individuals are integrated into society, rather than isolated atomistically. The overview of the politics of revolt presented earlier shows that the connectivity provided by the Internet is not the same as social capital, but that it holds potential as a form of networking, which is an essential component of social capital. Secondly, a communication system is needed that allows the social movements emerging from such networking to engage in self-reflection and to nurture self-awareness, crucial to consolidating networks, into more stable social identities. For this to occur, these communication systems need to be a source of stable content, which is open to contextualisation and aggregation and in which symbolic content is visually presented to its consumers.

Stable content

In the case of the imagined community of the nation, as presented by Anderson,[21] the daily press was once the primary communications medium through which its individual members' imagination was prompted. Newspapers could convey the core concepts of nationhood to its readers in a fairly stable, structured, coherent and consistent manner. In their writings the editors could establish the criteria of membership to the nation, whether civic, cultural or based on innate criteria. Readers could also find information about the symbols of nationhood and partake (if, for some, only vicariously) in the celebration thereof. These core concepts were presented as a given and made available only to members of the nation as if they were public goods. These goods become public (within the nation) to the extent that they met the requirements of inclusiveness ('they must be available to everyone if they are available to anyone'[22]) and jointness of supply ('consumption by some individuals does not preclude consumption by other').[23]

Dynamic contextualisation and aggregation

Although the core concepts of the nation were stabilised, their ability to connect with the reader was found, *inter alia*, by putting this conceptual framework into action on a daily basis so allowing for both stability and flexibility. This occurred when the interests of the daily readers were attuned, by the editors of the day, to those of the nation. Their task was to present the challenges of achieving and holding onto national self-determination in a way that resonated with the context of the daily lives of its readers, which then made it possible for readers to imagine themselves within the 'big picture' and to reflect on themselves as part of the larger scheme of things. This process amounted to the kind of information processing that entails the early steps in interest aggregation. The nationalist political party would then take this process further.

Symbolic representation

Hard-copy printed newspapers of both text and photographs give the reader a tangible, visual expression of the concepts, symbols, interests and context of the nation, in a form that is present as a constant reference point, which can be updated daily. News-reporting, through still photography, evolved into more than just a career skill, but became one of *the* art forms of the twentieth century. The methodology presented in the previous chapter entails a screen-based presentation of such a gauge of public opinion, which need *not* be based only on graphs and bar charts, but can and should be able to be *visualised* in many more ways.

DOI: 10.1057/9781137496195.0010

The scatter-gram presentation used in this study is but one more way of visualising and imagining the mass expression of interests.[24]

The nation has been the primary imagined community of those democracies that have been embedded in the institutional framework of the state and state-system. This need not be so in the democracies of the future. As is already apparent, contemporary societies are confronting some very large problems such as rapid global climate change, which extend far beyond the jurisdiction of any and every state. Larger units of decision-making will be required to confront these problems. Other problems, such as that of social cohesion, may be smaller than the jurisdiction of some states, and smaller decision-making units might be more appropriate to deal with these issues. So both larger and smaller units of democracy need to be envisaged, and some may not even be territorially bound, where the social unit of the nation may not be relevant or functional.[25] All of this will require yet more nimble imagination and more symbolic coherence if these socially constructed entities are to gain durability.

It could be argued that the quantitative sentiment analysis presented in Chapter 4 represents an early pioneering step in approximating these three properties. The data processing done in Chapter 4 is, in the first instance, an aggregation of statements that express preferences for and against democracy into stable, manageable categories. In future, depending on other issues that circulate in social media, other such analyses of affective sentiments can also be arranged in categories different to those presented here. To the extent that such analyses are replicated with the same or functionally equivalent categories, this categorisation is an early step in the standardisation of the conceptual dimensions of the issues at hand. As software develops, analyses should be able to show the dimensions (themes) of opinion, the width and depth of sentiment (how many supporters, and where they are located), the range of interests (the number of categories and where applicable) and the salience of various preferences.

Newspapers affected contextualisation and interest aggregation through snapshots of events in daily life, repeated on a daily basis, which, when combined, produced an on-going, if stuttering, contextual analysis. Our study is also a single snapshot. Should more advanced software enable a real-time aggregation of such interests within context, it would make such interest presentation more durable and fluid, even if not fixed. This can serve to act as a constant marker of social identity and a sense of community, imagined on the basis of an articulation of millions of distinct expressions of interests. In addition, demands are merged, through software, into an aggregated, yet fluid and dynamic, but more or less coherent public opinion.

Finally, one crucial cognitive process in the formation of imagined communities is that of self-reflection. As Castells noted with the Occupy... movement, such reflection centres on self-definition: who they are; what they stand for; what they want to be; and what they do not want to be. In their case, Internet blogs and chat rooms on social media provided both the platform for discussion and the raw data about themselves. Our methodology allows for new kinds of data about themselves to be generated, data that can complement the qualitative material found in blogs, and in this way it can facilitate this process of self-reflection – one of the most vital links in creating new imagined communities.

Our methodology is, of course, neutral with regard to the question of whether the politics of revolt should proceed outside or inside the established channels of participation. Self-reflection by interest groups going the conventional way can also be enhanced through data gathered by means of the sentiment analysis we demonstrate in this study.

The Internet: future impact

While the dramatic social networking events of the Arab Spring are evident in the form of direct action, there is also another, potentially far-reaching effect of the digital screen-based media that may be emerging, but in a less tangible, less easily observable and a possibly more insidious form, with its impact yet to be fully realised. This is the way that the Internet-based screen-media might impact on the process by which the human brain is shaped to form the mind, unique to every individual identity.

Personal identity

The concept of the mind as the personalised brain is central to the typology of personal identity profiles developed by neuroscientist Susan Greenfield.[26] She starts with the well-known property of neuronal plasticity exhibited by the human brain. This is found, *inter alia*, in the neural connections within the brain, some of which can become stronger and others weaker as the brain is exposed to different kinds of stimuli. As

DOI: 10.1057/9781137496195.0010

each individual brain is exposed to stimuli, by way of life experiences that are unique to that person, Greenfield shows how these connections take on a distinct pattern, illustrated, by way of example, among London taxi drivers. And she presents experimental data of how the neural connections of people who play the piano, and those who even just think about playing the piano (none of whom can actually play the instrument) differ from those of the control group – who do neither. The unique mind, she argues, is shaped in this way by the experiences that are specific to every individual, and the individual identity is found in the patterns of connections in the brain that emerge as some connections grow stronger than others. These experiences can be either direct or vicarious, by imagining events, situations or experiences of other (fictional) persons, as is the case when reading a novel.

One proactive way of shaping the neural circuits of the brain is through learning, whether it is memorising the roads of London by taxi drivers, mastering the piano or any other type of accomplishment that requires rigorous application of physical and cognitive abilities. Learning *is* the lifelong process of formation and re-formation of connections between brain cells in a deliberate, selected and structured form, thus moulding the plasticity of the brain in a particular, specific way reflective of what is absorbed. Learning is a lifelong process of building a framework of understanding through metaphors and symbols, which enables the brain to assign meaning (to grasp one less familiar thing in terms of another, more familiar thing),[27] which enhances understanding (to make a connection between two disparate and distinct entities, in the light of accumulated experience and information, using this conceptual framework of metaphors and symbols).[28] This is a process that takes time, is about presenting the brain with unambiguous uncontested input and which relies on repetition.

The impact of psychoactive drugs on the brain, according to Greenfield, can be understood in these terms. Synapses are the neural connections between brain cells through which communication within the brain takes place. Dopamine is a well-known natural transmitter that facilitates such communication, while serotonin is another one that suppresses such communication. The common expression of 'losing your mind', or the more contemporary one of 'blowing your mind', refers to a process of interference with this communications process, either by exaggerating or inhibiting it. For example, cannabis, according to Greenfield, can modify synapses and hence the communication between brain cells, and with it

DOI: 10.1057/9781137496195.0010

the plasticity within the brain. Apart from 'tripping out' – the immediate sense of well-being induced by this drug is also measurable in general de-motivation, loss of memory, shortened attention span and loss of the kind of co-ordination skills one needs to drive a car. The amphetamine called 'speed' also acts by increasing levels of dopamine, thus leading to dramatically increased levels of communication so often experienced as hallucinations. Heroin results in an even more radical intervention into these communication grids.

The first personal identity profile drawn by Greenfield is described as 'Someone'. Here the mind is your identity as seen by yourself (first person), while personality is your identity as others (third person) see it and assess you on the basis of traits expressed by you during social interaction with others. The personalisation of neural networks through a cultivation of the sense of self has been facilitated by the recognition that the lives of other people could be imagined. This process is closely tied to the emergence of the novel as literary genre. Here the reader could, in a second-hand way, experience the lives of fictional characters in a subjective way unlike any other previous stories. The personal detail of their lives, their emotional struggles and woes, their intimate relations and their social circumstances were now made available to the reader as entertainment, to be enjoyed in his/her own privacy. This vicarious experience has made for the capacity to visualise the lives of others and, following from that, to develop the capacity for empathy and compassion.[29] By immersing his/herself into the identity of the fictional character, the reader then also becomes more aware of his/her own personal traits and of the contrast between the two.

The construction of the self could then proceed against the more easily visualised reference point of other people, real or imaginary. This is crucial to the concept of becoming Someone: it entails the process of having 'to define yourself by the way others treat you', and 'the promotion of the self against others'.[30] The precise contours of the mind of Someone are then filled in through many information inputs, ranging from formal education through to popular culture and personal life experiences.

In its acute form, Someone is self-centred to the point of over-indulgence in some of the most basic human motivations. For Greenfield, these are aptly summarised in the Seven Deadly Sins: Anger, Gluttony, Lust, Sloth, Avarice, Vanity and Envy. Each of these indulgences is the result of individual excesses in the pursuit of social ranking and personal esteem and of the search for positive recognition for the self from others. However, because social status is relational, there is no safe and secure mark of achievement, no definitive end-goal of status security. Instead, the obverse applies: in a society of Someones, status anxiety is a perennial condition and depression a likely result. Following on from this perspective, at the bottom end of the ranking order are those with no status, and therefore no identity, and such an individual cannot be Someone but rather the very opposite – a Nobody. If for Nobodies, status cannot be conclusively captured and secured, then escape from this relentlessly competitive world can be found into the well-known avenue of psychoactive drugs or, as Greenfield suggests, now also into the parallel cyber-world.[31]

The personality profile of the Nobody, constructed by Greenfield, emerged from her interpretation of the impact of current digital media and its attendant 'screen culture', and on the possible or even likely future impact of such technologies. For her, 'the crucial issue boils down to the brain and how it adapts to screen technology. Familiar as I am with the malleability of the human brain, I predict that spending so much time in cyberspace will inevitably lead to minds very different from any others in human history'.[32]

The first potentially adverse impact of screen technology, she considers, is the conceivable effect it has on the cognitive processes of learning and understanding. Vicarious screen experiences, unlike those derived from book reading, are presented with the visual imagery of the events, characters and situations already completed on behalf of the viewer. The need for imagining these stories falls away, thus inhibiting creative thinking. She contends that viewing, rather than reading, makes for an experience rather than for thinking. Furthermore, such screen-based presentations provide symbolic material, but without the necessary conceptual framework within which to locate such symbols or with which to construct metaphors from these symbols. These icons then stand alone, without being buttressed by the required knowledge to make sense of them or to understand what they stand for.[33]

Secondly, Greenfield maintains, screen-based experiences tend towards becoming a solitary activity, a phenomenon closely observed by Putnam in his study of the TV generation of the 1970s,[34] thus contributing to the social isolation, even within households, of the individual. Second-hand experience, then, crowds out first-hand experience and interpersonal relationships.

DOI: 10.1057/9781137496195.0010

Screen-based computer games, according to Greenfield, add yet a new dimension to the impact of screen technology. Here, she argues, is a new activity that again gravitates against activating learning and gaining understanding.[35]

What, in essence, is it about the process of playing such games that makes them so dangerous? Greenfield presents it this way. Citing *World of Warcraft* as an example, she argues that such computer games are constructed of an almost unending series of tasks assigned to a player, which, on successful completion, is followed by a reward, which is consistently delivered with machine-driven precision and efficiency. Tasks are assigned to and executed by an avatar, a fictitious character representing the player in the game. Avatars inhabit the game but do so as empty shells, to be filled with identity attributes by the player, as he/she gains rewards. One of the attractions of this built-in task/reward structure is this very predictability over that of the real world. Yet life, very often, is not fair. To use two sporting metaphors: playing fields are not always level, but could tilt away from you, and the bounce of the ball might not always be in your favour. Invariably, however, these games are fair.

With reward goes a certain amount of pleasure. Pleasure, in turn, is closely linked to the release of endorphins, natural opiates in the body that act as transmitters in certain parts of the body. Their effect on the brain is to suspend temporarily the sense-of-self, to experience the immediate only, and at higher levels, to experience euphoria. This, Greenfield considers, is not unlike the effect of the release of an excessive amount of dopamine on the brain. Addictive drugs could have this effect, and such an overload of dopamine could affect a partial shutdown of parts of the communication lines in the brain, which could cause exclusion of the sense of both past and future, a concomitant strengthening of the perception of the immediate and of process over content. This leads Greenfield to her central hypothesis about the addictive effect of some kinds of computer games (without implicating any particular game). This proves that computer games could have a similar effect on the brain as is the case with psychoactive drugs in inducing an excessive release of dopamine on the brain. Following from that, she elaborates the hypothesis that repeated playing of such games may lead to the re-configuring of the brain in a way that stimulates further excessive dopamine release, which then can become addictive, leading the person to indulge in yet more computer games.[36]

DOI: 10.1057/9781137496195.0010

This addiction follows from the re-arrangement of the neural connections that favour this task/reward/pleasure sequence over the mind, which consists of the unique personalised conceptual framework and attendant neural maps – the source of personal identity. What remains is the individual, as the passive recipient of the machine-delivered stimulus/reward process, engaged in the mindless thinking of the 'depersonalized hedonism of screen technology' – a Nobody.[37]

The third identity profile Greenfield identifies is that of Anyone. Here, collective identity trumps that of the individual, whose uniqueness is suppressed and displaced by a personal identity derived from collectively shared beliefs – either religious or secular. These belief systems are, in their acute forms, fundamentalist, and contain rigid convictions of what comprises the 'Truth' and which prescribe from adherents specific actions in both private and public behaviour. For Greenfield, the question is whether commitment to such a total belief system can change a person's brain and, therefore, mind and, therefore, identity.

The findings she reports indicate that 'true believers'[38] are affected most in terms of their emotions. Of the core emotions of anger, fear, happiness, sadness, surprise and disgust, it is the latter that appears to be most strongly present. When disgust is expressed towards any object, it stimulates protective inclinations to the extent that exclusion from the realm of influence emanating from the source of disgust is activated. Within the world of ideas, the non-believer, the heretic, the impure, the enemy, the foreigner, the outsider is perceived as repugnant and warrants not only to be isolated, but in extreme situations – to be exterminated. Within the brain, strong defences need to be constructed by 'closing the mind' in a metaphorical sense. Collective on-going endorsement and reinforcement of centrally held beliefs on the one hand, and the hostile exclusion of competing ideas from elsewhere, are key to reinforcing the identity of Anyone.[39]

The strength of convictions is, according to Greenfield, to be understood in terms of the resilience of the neuronal connections within the brain. The 'use or lose it' rule applies. The brain mechanism of long-term potentiation (LPT) enables connections between synapses to strengthen the more they are used. The process of achieving such 'super-neuronal connectivity' within a collective, that is, conformity of convictions at a high level of intensity is well-known. The repertoire includes: (i) repetition of the content of the belief system through rituals, preferably low in frequency but high in its capacity for emotional arousal; (ii) collective

DOI: 10.1057/9781137496195.0010

chanting; (iii) moving in synchronisation; (iv) traumatic initiation rites; (v) the use of music; and (vi) the use of a sacred text as a fixed reference point for anchoring convictions, whether it is located in the Bible, the Koran, the writings of Marx and Engels or the sayings of Mao Zedong. Those most susceptible would be (i) the youth; (ii) those who do not have access to competing ideas with which to challenge these truth claims; and (iii) where reinforcement is consistently applied. These shared experiences, may, according to Greenfield, activate the release of endorphins, key to the suppression of pain and to activate a sense of well-being.[40]

In a society comprising a critical mass of Anyones, the dynamics of competition for status and identity experienced by individual Someones repeats itself at the collective level. The collective unit is perpetually engaged in asserting its worth against that of the enemy, comprising other, foreign, hostile outsiders. This is done by elevating the collective self, and denigrating the outsiders as a way of establishing positive distinctiveness for the own group.[41] In this process, the Seven Deadly Sins tend to be repeated at the collective level, an extravagant over-indulgence in the pursuit of superiority, an expression of collective esteem and self-centredness. Anger, directed at the loathsome and inferior out-group, becomes the dominant form of expressing the collective identity of Anyone.

In a nutshell, the acute versions of each profile consist of the following attributes. In the case of the personal identity profile of Someone, the substantive content of identity is individualised; in the case of Anyone it is standardised; and in the case of Nobody it is empty. Someone derives identity from relational status assigned to the individual, which is acquired through a dynamic competitive evaluation by others. Likewise, Anyone derives it from relative group status, derived from the contest for collective esteem, in which the own-group asserts its worth over the despised out-group proactively, with reference to the validation of itself typically found in sacred texts. Nobodies derive identity not from competitive striving, but from entertainment, from playing certain kinds of computer games, in which the player is anonymous, docile and reactive in accepting the identity of the avatar that is virtual, written into the scripted programme of the game and experienced through the electronic screen. In their acute forms, being Someone brings 'individuality without fulfilment'; being Anyone yields 'fulfilment without individuality'; and being Nobody brings 'neither individuality nor fulfilment'.[42] Acquisition of the identity of Someone is status dependent;

DOI: 10.1057/9781137496195.0010

that of Anyone is ideology dependent; and that of Nobody is machine dependent.

Personal identity and regime types

This typology of identity profiles resonates with much of the standard literature in political science on the social base of specific regime types, some of which are reviewed in Chapter 2. The mild version of the profile of Someone can be recognised in the archetypal citizen of the Civic Culture. This individual knows what he/she wants, can rank-order these preferences and is confident that he/she will be able to act together with like-minded co-citizens to successfully pursue these interests. Such goal-directed behaviour is, however, constrained by various factors so that unfettered and even narcissistic self-centeredness does not prevail. These include: (i) the mutual obligations of reciprocity inherent to social capital; (ii) cross-cutting social ties; (iii) the conviction that the individual is embedded in a society comprising both a private and a public space and even a public sphere; and (iv) an imagined community with an overarching social identity which is a focus of loyalty and patriotism.

The acute version of Someone is the individual bent on pursuing his/her own interests on the basis of a narrowly defined rationality. This Someone is arguably found in the individual that undercuts the strength of collective action through persistent free riding. It is, above all, the individual who pursues own profit at the expense of the commons, irrespective of costs and consequences, leading to the eventual destruction thereof.[43]

The profile of Anyone can be recognised in both its mild and acute forms. In its mild form it is the individual who imagines her/himself to be a member of a nation, which in turn, is usually embedded within the institutional and geographical framework of the state. National identity configured in this form is, for a large part, compatible with the personality profile of Someone, also in its mild form. The individual who identifies with the civic nation, and who is also a citizen to whom is assigned the rights and obligations of membership to a liberal democracy epitomises this combination. As identified by Greenfield, Anyone in its acute form is the individual who finds like-minded associates within the ranks of secular or religious fundamentalist movements. Here, collective identity completely shuts out that of the individual, making it entirely incompatible with the identity profile of Someone, in either its mild or acute forms.

DOI: 10.1057/9781137496195.0010

Nobodies are shaped by psychoactive drugs and/or, in the hypothesis of Greenfield, by certain kinds of computer games. Drug use goes back deep into human history and prehistory, while computer games are the product of the Digital Age alone. Nevertheless, some conceptual recognition can be found between Greenfield's profile of a Nobody and the individuals that make up the mass society as understood by Kornhauser (outlined in Chapter 2). In this society (characteristic of continental Europe up to the end of the Second World War), individuals and/or nuclear households become socially isolated by virtue of the socially destructive effects of massive, rapid, industrial modernisation and its attendant social disloca- tion. Coupled to that was the devastation of both the First and Second World Wars. Such atomism is the first step in the creation of conditions of self-estrangement, key to becoming a Nobody ready to be mobilised into a totalitarian society along the Soviet Communist and European Fascist models. Once the totalitarian regime is secured, the further project is to change the identities of these citizens once more, this time into true believers: loyal, subservient, fundamentalist and enthusiastic Anyones.

Greenfield's typology also allows us to gain more insight into this process of totalitarian imposition, especially with insights from a new work on the Chinese totalitarian experience by Frank Dikötter, *The Tragedy of Liberation. A History of the Chinese Revolution 1945–57*. Dikötter describes how Mao gained control of various provinces of China as the Second World War reached its end, and the Japanese invasion was defeated. Manchuria was one such key region, and here, Mao claimed to be following the revolutionary peasantry, who were taking the initiative in displacing the remaining military presence of the nationalist forces of Chiang Kai-shek. In May 1946, Mao issued instructions for an unre- strained class struggle to be initiated in the countryside.

Using data from recently released official party archives, Dikötter chal- lenges the notion of a spontaneous uprising by the exploited peasants against their landlords. The reality was very different. Rural pre-com- munist China was composed of a patchwork of owners, part-owners and leaseholders, who were knit together in villages with extended mutual contractual obligations that were built up over generations, stretching back over centuries. Very few were completely landless labourers.

This social fabric was now to be shredded. Party cadres went from village to village executing a meticulously planned programme of terror. First, villagers were allocated to officially designated classes: landlord, rich peasant, middle-class peasant, poor peasant or labourer. These group

DOI: 10.1057/9781137496195.0010

identities were coercively imposed, mostly arbitrarily, even randomly, and had little, if anything, to do with the imagined reality of those classified as such, but everything to do with that of the party cadres. Then those designated as poor peasants were urged 'to turn hardship into hatred'. Under pressure, some individuals aired genuine grievances, others were invented. Both were amplified at countless 'speak bitterness' public meetings. Some of the accusers were swept up and became zealous revolutionary true believers, expecting something larger than life to be unfolding in the creation of a new and better era.

Once polarisation had been manufactured, further 'struggle meetings' were conducted, where victims were denounced, scorned, insulted, humiliated, tortured and in some cases, executed in public. Even children, if they ended up being classified as 'little landlords', fell victim to this process. The rewards for the accusers were immediate: the assets of the victims were distributed among the accusers. In this way, the villagers who acted as accusers became co-perpetrators of the terror and accomplices in murder. By the start of 1948, through these methods, the communists had established control over 160 million people in the countryside, and roughly between 500,000 and one million people were executed or had committed suicide.[44]

Shortly after this campaign, the communists seized the centre of power, and on 1 October 1949, at a rally in Beijing, Mao declared that the Central Peoples Government had been formed. The next phase in the securing of control unfolded in the cities, mostly against internal 'counter-revolutionaries'. Almost every public bureaucracy in every province was purged, and many of the detained, accused and convicted ended up in vast labour camps or Gulags. Here the process of totalitarian conversion went to another level. Indoctrination sessions (called 'thought reform') were held in these prison camps on a daily basis for years on end. The basic procedure was for the accused to confess (to wrong thoughts), and then to publicly denounce themselves for such thoughts and/or acts. Once meetings were concluded, inmates had to continue denouncing one another in their cells. The process became omnipresent with no respite. This became, according to one former inmate, 'a carefully cultivated Auschwitz of the mind'. One of Dikötter's interviewees was Robert Ford, a British citizen, who endured this for four years. His eloquent recollection is that:

> When you're being beaten up, you can turn into yourself and find a corner of your mind in which to fight the pain. But when you're being spiritually

DOI: 10.1057/9781137496195.0010

tortured by thought reform, there's nowhere you can go. It affects you at the most profound, deepest level and attacks your very identity.[45]

Another interviewee, a former nationalist military officer, recounts that thought reform was experienced as nothing short of the 'physical and mental liquidation of oneself by oneself'.[46] Dikötter concludes: 'Those who resisted the process committed suicide. Those who survived it renounced being themselves'.[47] The objective of totalitarian terror was comprehensively achieved: the unique personal identity of being Someone was abandoned by the targets of thought reform themselves, and they embraced the emptiness of being Nobody as the only means to physical survival.

The changing social base

Can the political significance of atomistic self-estranged individuals, of such Nobodies in the democratic politics of the early twenty-first century, be the same as was the case in early twentieth century in Europe? Further, can the threat of totalitarian regime-change within both the global centre and the periphery of democratic regimes be similar to what it was in the previous century?

For one, the Nobodies of the current era are being created, not through massive socio-economic upheavals, compounded by the global modern total industrial warfare between the superpowers of the day. Even the 2008 Financial Crisis and the political impact of the subsequent Great Recession are not of the scale of the 1929 Great Crash and Depression. In the Greenfield hypothesis, these twenty-first-century Nobodies are being formed through a process of recreation, of playing certain kinds of computer games, which is one of *the* sources of entertainment within the screen culture of this age. It is a form of self-indulgence that is voluntarily engaged in, at the core of modern capitalist consumer culture, and not the result of huge social forces or malevolent political coercion. Leaving aside the impact of psychoactive drugs, what can be more mainstream and more innocuous than that?

In addition, the Greenfield hypothesis is, in any case, strenuously opposed by some analysts, few more energetically than Jane McGonigal as evident from the title of her book *Reality Is Broken – Why Games Make Us Better, and How They Can Change the World*.[48] The question about the extent to which these role-playing Internet-based games that are at the core of the screen culture will eventually affect the social isolation of players will

DOI: 10.1057/9781137496195.0010

be settled only in the future as this technology plays itself out. So too will the question of to what extent the personal identities of the avatars will displace those of the individual players themselves, becoming surrogates for the real thing and so turning them into Nobodies. Furthermore, there also remains the question of the extent to which the connectivity of the Internet can contribute the growth of bridging social capital.[49] Given the aforementioned, it seems reasonable at this stage to allow for the personality profile of Nobody to be conceptualised as a variable, which like that of Someone or Anyone, can manifest itself in a milder or more acute form, and that the milder it is, the more compatible it becomes with the other two types, as part of a multidimensional personal identity profile.

Opium of the people

What appears to be uncontested is the claim about the addictive power of these games. The games that interest McGonigal display the following structure: they (i) are entered into voluntarily; (ii) set clear goals of what is to be achieved; (iii) uphold rules that direct behaviour and set limits to strategic options; (iv) entail the overcoming of obstacles at a level selected by the player; and (v) activate a feedback system where success, or even just effort, is rewarded.[50]

What makes these games so compelling and addictive is that they can test the player to his/her limit of ability and provide immediate rewards for achievement. When such challenging obstacles are overcome, the neural centres in the brain that underlie the sensation of pleasure are activated. In presenting this defence of games, McGonigal affirms the importance of process over content, and emphasises the emotional gratification experienced by players who accomplish challenging tasks, and who then promptly receive rewards, delivered with machine-driven precision. She recounts her experience of playing *World of Warcraft (WoW)* as akin to the effect of being on a morphine drip line: work and reward is delivered consistently and predictably, and although the 'work' is unreal the emotional rewards of pleasure and sense of achievement is real, which to her, is what matters most.[51]

Although there are many critical shortcomings in the structure of these games that disqualify them from being metaphors for life as we know it, that does not appear to concern McGonigal. Her agenda is to make the case for restructuring activities in real life to replicate the pleasure generating the cognitive format of these games.[52]

DOI: 10.1057/9781137496195.0010

To consider the possible social and political impact of the growth of such a screen-based games culture, one has to locate it within the broader context of the changing social and economic base of modern capitalist democracies. The contours of the 'new economy' identified by Bennett (see Chapter 2) in his 1998 paper are now becoming more sharply etched. According to one report[53] from *The Economist*, mature capitalist economies are undergoing what can be described as no less than a profound technological transformation, similar to the Industrial Revolution, which moved the production of wealth from agriculture to industry. A century ago, about one-third of the American labour force worked on farms, today less than 2 per cent remain in that sector. This pattern repeated itself in Britain, with the new technology producing much 'creative' destruction. In this process, many skills became obsolete, as machines took over from craftsmen. The immediate dislocation resulting from this technological unemployment was not just in the labour market, but also had a wide-ranging social impact. In the longer term, over the course of the twentieth century, according to this report, the initial gains in wealth went to the owners of capital, but labour eventually caught up, and the loss in jobs was largely reversed with expanded employment in the industrial and later in the service sectors.

According to this same report, the Keynesian prediction of technological unemployment is now, 30 years into the digital revolution, again relevant. The early indicators of such a transformation are found, firstly, in the increasing wealth that accrues to the owners of capital – a trend that is common knowledge by now. In the United States, the share of the top 1 per cent of income earners has risen from 9 per cent in the 1970s to 22 per cent in 2014. Secondly, at the bottom end of the income bracket, unemployment in the 'rich world' is rising. Thirdly, machines, driven by the rise of computing power, for many years increasing at the exponential rate described by Moore's Law, are taking over many previously secure jobs. The report cites one study that predicts that 47 per cent of established occupational categories are at risk of being automated. The logic of the new technology is that any work that can be made routine and codified can also be automated. Fourthly, new firms emerge that employ a minute labour force. Instagram, for example, just before being sold to Facebook, had 30 million customers and employed 13 people. By contrast, Kodak, recently bankrupted, employed 145,000 people at its peak.

The social and political implications are readily seen. At the one end, rising inequality featuring a super-rich elite who masters new technology

DOI: 10.1057/9781137496195.0010

and also creates it; a middle class under threat; and an expanding lower class – the latter two being the perennial losers in the contest with new technology. *The Economist* report forecasts that this decline of the middle class, historically the social base of the Civic Culture 'could generate a more antagonistic, unstable and potentially dangerous politics'.[54]

This is a view that would gain much endorsement from mainstream political science, but the contrarian forecast by Tyler Cowen is worth considering.[55] Writing about the United States only, in line with the aforementioned forecast, he anticipates a major decline in the size of the middle class, with a new economic and social bifurcation, not of 1 per cent against 99 per cent, but rather 15 per cent against the remaining 85 per cent. The top 15 per cent, he says, will be a cognitive elite, an extreme meritocracy, those who create the new technology, who are able to work with these intelligent machines and who are able to find synergy between the capacities of machines and those human capacities resistant to auto-mation.[56] They will not only be exceedingly wealthy but also a coherent social formation, politically well-networked with strong bonding social capital. They will be highly skilled in protecting their interests – primarily their wealth – and the economic base from which it derives.

The bottom 85 per cent, by contrast, will comprise the technologically unemployed or underemployed, those with 'bulls**t jobs', as anthropolo-gist David Graeber describes it.[57] This 'new underclass', in Cowen's termi-nology, will in future (and are already) most likely move to states such as Texas with available low-cost housing, where services are cheap and of low quality, and where jobs can be found. In effect, the rapid growth of large, new high-end shantytowns are foreseen. This underclass will not, in Cowen's view, be subsidised all the way by the top 15 per cent with social welfare. Such welfare expenditure is likely to stagnate, but real wages for the 85 per cent will be allowed to decline.[58]

This is a social base that is not conducive to the maintenance of demo-cratic regimes. But Cowen anticipates that this society of high inequal-ity is not likely to be politically unstable, with endemic social protest against their particular conditions – or against democracy itself. Instead, he finds reason to think that it will be relatively peaceful. The factor inducing such pacification is identified only with a few fleeting remarks about 'cheap fun', and a paraphrasing of the infamous remark attributed to Queen Marie Antoinette on the eve of the French Revolution. When being told that mass protests were driven by people desperate for bread, her rejoinder was 'let them eat cake'.[59] Cowen's advice to a government

DOI: 10.1057/9781137496195.0010

intent on maintaining social control over the new underclass is then to 'let them watch Internet'.[60]

These oblique remarks make sense when considering the addictive qualities of the kind of fun available on the Internet through gaming, which is an industry already larger than Hollywood.[61] In a way then, Cowen allows for Internet-generated fun and pleasure to become the functional equivalent of the pacifying force Karl Marx attributed to organised religion in the capitalist states of his time, which he considered to be nothing less than 'the opium of the people'.[62] These screen-based pleasures can only become a pacifying force of such magnitude if they are able to turn citizens into subjects with some of the attributes of Nobodies: docile and quiescent, reactive rather than proactive, addicted and machine dependent.

Conclusion

In ideal democracies the criteria of both citizen effectiveness and of system capacity are met. The contemporary age registers a continuous theme of unease with representative democracy, the standard institutional device for achieving citizen effectiveness. The Internet revolution is also effecting fundamental changes to the social base of established democracies but in many ways is yet to materialise conclusively. As we argued earlier, this social upheaval is making it even more difficult to adequately represent citizens for the following reasons. Firstly, social media allows almost complete agency for the individual to express him/herself in a unique way, resulting in mass self-communication. Secondly, the up-to-now standardised collective identities in the form of the imagined communities of nation and citizen are eroded by both the global connectivity of the Internet-based communications network and the changing social base of established democracies. This makes the standard requirement for effective representation – that of interest articulation and interest aggregation – more complicated.

The survey of the views of selected analysts and of how the Internet-based technology is likely to impact in future on the personal and social lives of democratic citizens has allowed us to identify three attributes of a social base favourable to the establishment of new imagined communities in the Digital Age. The first being conditions favourable to the growth of social capital. The second being a communication system that

DOI: 10.1057/9781137496195.0010

generates stable but not static content, which allows for dynamic contextualisation and aggregation and for visual symbolic representation of the material needed for individuals to reflect on themselves and to imagine being part of a larger social entity. A third attribute is a cultural system that allows for individuals with the personal identity profiles of both Someone and Anyone (in their compatible milder versions) to flourish, and which allows for the presence of only a few but not a critical mass of Nobodies. The role of the Internet in such cultural dynamics remains a contested issue.

We can now, in conclusion, return to the larger question of popular culture and the Internet. From the review presented in this chapter, two indistinct yet starkly diverging prospects emerge for the kind of popular culture that the Internet can create. The first is closely associated with the interpretation made by Castells of the Occupy... movement. Here, the Internet is a site of revolt, one that can and has been removed from the symbolic public urban spaces that they have briefly occupied, but which is not entirely dismantled. They still do maintain a presence in the cyber world, or what Castells calls the 'autonomous space of flows', from which they cannot be dislodged because the Internet has become a network of networks, and according to him, beyond the reach of authorities trying to contain freedom of expression through balkanisation of the Internet and increasing comprehensive surveillance efforts.[63] The Internet, then, is a site of empowerment for self-reflection and of self-assertion from where the long-term objective is to re-assert values of equality, multiculturalism, participation, deliberation and open communication with the end objective, no less, of re-inventing democracy.[64]

The second interpretation draws on the work of Greenfield and Cowen. In their view, the social impact of the Internet, which Castells describes as being that of individuation and autonomy, is instead interpreted as isolation and atomisation. Virtual social contact, an empty form of social interaction, increasingly crowds out the real thing, which is filled with the chemistry of emotion and physical presence. Gaming and social media sites are considered to be primary agents in this process. The dominant content of the Internet is at best, that of hedonistic entertainment, that not only inhibits the growth of personal identities and social intelligence needed to assert individuals as autonomous social and political actors, but at worst, serves as the functional equivalent of an anaesthetic, an opiate that dulls the senses of thought, understanding and critical thinking. The Internet, then, in this perspective is becoming

DOI: 10.1057/9781137496195.0010

a site where people do not mobilise for revolt, but rather, where they are disempowered in terms of the growth of personal identity and of social and political influence.

Which way will it go? One way of weighing up these two scenarios is to take a look at what has gone before in the Internet revolution and how that measures up to the predictions of that time. This is what renowned futurist Karl Albrecht has done in his recent article 'The Information Revolution's Broken Promises'.[65] His general contention is that, as with most – if not all – previous technological revolutions, unanticipated and unwanted consequences have now emerged some 20 years into this revolution. He lists some eight predictions made then, to show how wrong they were and then updates each prediction. Those of immediate relevance will be discussed here.

Two predictions about the structure of the Internet economy can be grouped together: Firstly, 'The Internet will create a "New Economy" with more space for new entrepreneurs, and a "wider, flatter, more democratized marketplace"'; and secondly, 'Digital technologies will narrow the Wealth Gap'. Both predictions, according to Albrecht, have proved horribly wrong. The Internet economy has turned out to be much like the old economy, with a small number of mega-firms dominating the sector, relentlessly squeezing out new entrants. And, the wealth gap has not narrowed, but has gone the other way. As we have discussed in this book, Albrecht notes that many middle-class jobs have been lost, real wages have stagnated and massive profits have accrued at the top in the hands of executives and share-holders. This confirms one of the threads of the argument presented in this book: that the social base of democracy has been dramatically changed.

Another prediction assessed by Albrecht, which also holds implications for the informed citizen and one that should be the foundation of the Civic Culture, is: 'The Internet Will Make Us Better Informed'. Instead, argues Albrecht, news channels, in cut-throat competition with one another, have dumbed down their information with ever more degenerate attention-seeking packages in what has become a race to the bottom: 'violence, conflict, vulgarity, voyeurism and gratuitous use of sex'.

Two further predictions that failed to materialise also align with arguments presented in this book: 'The Internet Will Create a World Community'; and 'The Internet Will Spread Democracy'. According to Albrecht, the 'community' that has been created is shallow, torn by

DOI: 10.1057/9781137496195.0010

factionalism and promotes atomisation. He endorses the Schmidt and Cohen assessment of internet mobilisation against dictators (they have been easier to dislodge, than to replace with democratic regimes) and considers the loss of privacy a decisive blow against established democracies.

These unintended consequences tend to tilt the overall direction of our Internet future away from secure democratic societies and closer to a less pleasant, less attractive, if not murky future, with diminished citizen effectiveness – unless, as Albrecht maintains, a 'grand correction' is made. In a similar vein, Schmidt and Cohen also call for a new social contract to stabilise the rights of democratic citizens and to domesticate this new technology.[66]

Technology itself might become a useful ingredient of this social contract. The central argument of this book is that the Internet-based social media provide a radical new technology for the articulate expression of interests, which, in tandem with new data analysis methods, can be used for executing the first steps for aggregating these interests and for expanding collective self-awareness through self-reflection – key to the construction of new imagined communities.

Notes

1   E. Schmidt and J. Cohen (2013) *The New Digital Age. Reshaping the Future of People, Nations and Business* (New York: Alfred A. Knopf), p. 4.

2   P.J. Schraeder and H. Redissi (2011) 'Ben Ali's Fall', *Journal of Democracy*, 22(3), 5–19.

3   M. Castells (2012) *Networks of Outrage and Hope. Social Movements in the Internet Age* (Cambridge, UK: Polity Press), p. 28.

4   T. Masoud (2011) 'The Road to (and from) Liberation Square', *Journal of Democracy*, 22(3), 20–34. For more on the role of the digital media in the events in both Tunisia and Egypt, see P.N. Howard and M. Hussain (2011) 'The Role of the Digital Media', *Journal of Democracy*, 22(3), 35–48.

5   *The Economist*, 22–28 October 2011, 70.

6   G.A. Almond and G.B. Powell (1966) *Comparative Politics. A Developmental Approach* (Boston: Little, Brown & Co.), p. 98.

7   T.H. Sander and R.D. Putnam (2011) 'Still Bowling Alone? The Post-9/11 Split', *Journal of Democracy*, 21(1), 9–16.

8   N.J. Brown (2013) 'Egypt's Failed Transition', *Journal of Democracy*, 24(4), 45–58.

DOI: 10.1057/9781137496195.0010

9   Schmidt and Cohen, *The New Digital Age*, chapter 4.

10   Schmidt and Cohen, *The New Digital Age*, p. 127.

11   This concept is attributed to Henry Kissinger; see Schmidt and Cohen, *The New Digital Age*, p. 131.

12   Schmidt and Cohen, *The New Digital Age*, p. 148.

13   Schmidt and Cohen, *The New Digital Age*, chapter 2. See also L. Diamond (2010) 'Liberation Technology', *Journal of Democracy*, 21(3), 69–83; R. Deibert and R. Rohozinski (2010) 'Liberation vs. Control: The Future of Cyberspace', *Journal of Democracy*, 21(4), 43–57; R. MacKinnon (2011) 'China's "Networked Authoritarians"', *Journal of Democracy*, 22(2), 32–46; X. Qiang (2011) 'The Battle for the Chinese Internet', *Journal of Democracy*, 22(2), 47–61; E. Morozov (2011) 'Whither Internet Control?', *Journal of Democracy*, 22(2), 62–74.

14   The role of democratic regimes, and in this case the United States, in deploying extensive surveillance of its own citizens, as well as those of other democratic allies was exposed in 2013 by Edward Snowden, an IT specialist contracted by the US government. This lead to an open call to the US government by major Internet companies that such efforts should be rule-bound, narrowly tailored so that intervention is proportionate to risks, transparent and subject to oversight. This call was endorsed by AOL, Facebook, Google, Linkedin, Microsoft, Twitter and Yahoo. See http://reformgovernmentsurveillance.com. See also Schmidt and Cohen, *The New Digital Age*, chapters 2 and 3, and the blog of Bruce Schneier, 'The Battle for Power on the Internet' (Online, available at: https://www.schneier.co./blog/archives/2013/10/the _battle_for_1.html [04/11/2013]).

15   Castells, *Networks of Outrage and Hope*, pp. 179–184, 185.

16   Castells, *Networks of Outrage and Hope*, p. 227.

17   Castells, *Networks of Outrage and Hope*, pp. 188–191.

18   Castells, *Networks of Outrage and Hope*, p. 230.

19   Castells, *Networks of Outrage and Hope*, p. 231.

20   Castells, *Networks of Outrage and Hope*, pp. 225, 226. Used with permission from Polity Press.

21   B. Anderson (1983) *Imagined Communities*, revised edn. (London: Verso).

22   M. Olson, Jr., (1965) *The Logic of Collective Action. Public Goods and the Theory of Groups* (Cambridge MA: Harvard University Press), p. 14.

23   A. Rabushka and K.A. Shepsle (1972) *Politics in Plural Societies. A Theory of Democratic Instability*,(Columbus OH: Charles E. Merrill), p. 84.

24   One creative example of other forms of data presentation from which can be learnt is by PROCESSQ (Online, available at: http://ekisto.sq.ro [23/06/2014]).

25   R.A. Dahl and E.R. Tufte (1973) *Size and Democracy* (Stanford CA: Stanford University Press).

DOI: 10.1057/9781137496195.0010

26 S. Greenfield (2009) *Id. The Quest for Meaning in the 21st Century* (London: Hodder & Stoughton).

27 Greenfield, *Id*, p. 81.

28 Greenfield, *Id*, p. 167.

29 Greenfield, *Id*, p. 123. See also S. Pinker (2011) *The Better Angels of Our Nature. The Decline of Violence in History and Its Causes* (London: Penguin), pp. 172–188.

30 Greenfield, *Id*, pp. 152, 153.

31 Greenfield, *Id*, pp. 135–155.

32 Greenfield, *Id*, p. 160.

33 Greenfield, *Id*, pp. 155–190, at 178. Greenfield refers to the icon of the egg-timer as an example. This is a device, shaped like a symmetrical funnel which is constricted in the middle to allow for only a small connecting passage, and filled with sand, which in stationary form would collect at the bottom end of the funnel. This timer is activated by standing it on its head, thus letting the sand funnel downwards again. Every such device is built to a specific time that it takes for the sand to run down after being tilted over, becoming a timer for whatever need, such as timing how long to boil an egg. The figure of speech, about 'the sands of time running out' is derived from this gadget and denotes not just a timing mechanism, but also the concept of time as a precious commodity, the inevitability of time and events that run their course, and also of the irreversibility of such events.

34 R.D. Putnam (2000) *Bowling Alone. The Collapse and Revival of American Community* (New York: Simon & Schuster). R.D. Putnam (1995) 'Turning In, Tuning Out: The Strange Disappearance of Social Capital in America', *PS ,Political Science & Politics*, 28(4), 664–683.

35 Greenfield, *Id*, pp. 193,194.

36 Greenfield, *Id*, p. 202.

37 Greenfield, *Id*, pp. 203, 211.

38 The pioneering work in this field remains the book by E. Hoffer (1951) *The True Believer* (New York: Harper & Row, 1966 edition also by Harper & Row).

39 Greenfield, *Id*, pp. 211–231.

40 Greenfield, *Id*, pp. 233–251.

41 This claim is also central to social identity theory, a sub-field within political psychology. See L. Huddy (2003) 'Group Identity and Social Cohesion', in D.O. Sears, L. Huddy and R. Jervis (eds), *Oxford Handbook of Political Psychology* (New York: Oxford University Press), pp. 511–558.

42 Greenfield, *Id*, p. 254.

43 G. Hardin (1968) 'The Tragedy of the Commons', *Science*, 162, 1243–1248.

44 F. Dikötter (2013) *The Tragedy of Liberation. A History of the Chinese Revolution 1945-57* (London: Bloomsbury), p. 74.

DOI: 10.1057/9781137496195.0010

45   Dikötter, *The Tragedy of Liberation*, p. 248. ©Frank Dikötter, 2013, 'The Tragedy of Liberation', by permission of Bloomsbury Publishing.

46   Dikötter, *The Tragedy of Liberation*, p. 248.

47   Dikötter, *The Tragedy of Liberation*, p. 248.

48   J. McGonigal (2011) *Reality Is Broken. Why Games Make Us Better, and How They Can Change the World* (London: Jonathan Cape), p. 93.

49   McGonigal insists that multi-player social interaction games are in fact creating new social capital. See McGonigal, *Reality Is Broken*, p. 93. The more equivocal position is taken by Charles Murray: 'It depends'. See C. Murray (2013) *Coming Apart. The State of White America, 1960–2010* (New York: Crown Forum/Random House), p. 248.

50   McGonigal, *Reality Is Broken*, p. 21.

51   McGonigal, *Reality Is Broken*, p. 61.

52   Objections to this agenda are found in R.W. Spencer (2013) 'Work Is Not a Game', *Research Technology Management*, 56(6), 59–60.

53   Briefing: The Future of Jobs, *The Economist*, 18–24 January 2014, 18–21.

54   Briefing: The Future of Jobs, 23.

55   T. Cowen (2013) *Average Is Over. Powering America beyond the Age of the Great Stagnation* (New York: Penguin).

56   For data showing this trend in the United States from 1959 to 2009, and to what extent the wealthy represent a cognitive elite, see Murray, *Coming Apart*, pp. 49–68.

57   Briefing: The Future of Jobs, 18.

58   Cowen, *Average Is Over*, pp. 236.

59   A. Partington (ed.) (1996) *The Oxford Dictionary of Quotations*, revised 4th edn. (Oxford: Oxford University Press), p. 446.

60   Cowen, *Average Is Over*, p. 244.

61   Cowen, *Average Is Over*, p. 67.

62   Partington, *The Oxford Dictionary of Quotations*, p. 452.

63   Castells, *Networks of Outrage and Hope*, p. 222.

64   Castells, *Networks of Outrage and Hope*, pp. 244–246.

65   K. Albrecht (2014) 'The Information Revolution's Broken Promises', *The Futurist*, 48(2) (Online, available at: http://www.wfs.org/futurist/2014-issues-futurist/march-april-2014-vol-48-no-2/information-revolution%E2%80%99s-broken-promises [27/08/2014]).

66   Schmidt and Cohen, *The New Digital Age*, p. 257.

DOI: 10.1057/9781137496195.0010

Bibliography

AfroBarometer (2008) 'The Quality of Democracy
and Governance in Africa: New Results from
Afrobarometer Round 4', *Afrobarometer Network*.
Working Paper No. 108, http://www.afrobarometer.org/
files/documents/working_papers/AfropaperNo108.pdf,
date accessed 16/08/2012.
—— (2008a) *AfroBarometer Online Data Analysis*, http://
www.jdsurvey.net/afro/AnalizeSample.jsp, date
accessed 30/05/2012.

▶ Albrecht, K. (2014) 'The Information Revolution's Broken
Promises', *The Futurist*, 48(2), http://www.wfs.org/
futurist/2014-issues-futurist/march-april-2014-vol-48-
no-2/information-revolution%E2%80%99s-broken-
promises, date accessed 16/05/2014.

Allport, G. (1954) *The Nature of Prejudice* (Cambridge,
MA: Addison-Wesley).

Almond, G.A. and G.B. Powell (1966) *Comparative Politics.
A Developmental Approach* (Boston: Little, Brown &
Co.).

Almond, G.A. and S. Verba (1963) *The Civic Culture:
Political Attitudes and Democracy in Five Nations*
(London: SAGE Publications Ltd.).

Anderson, B. (2006) *Imagined Communities. Reflections on
the Origin and Spread of Nationalism* (London: Verso,
revised edn.).

AOL, Facebook, Google, Linkedin, Microsoft, Twitter and
Yahoo. See http://reformgovernmentsurveillance.com.

Arendt, H. (1951) *The Origins of Totalitarianism* (New York:
Harcourt, Brace and Company).

——(1963) *On Revolution* (London: Macmillan).

Asur, S. and B.A. Huberman (2010) 'Predicting the Future with Social Media', *Computers and Society* (Cornell University Computer Science Paper).

Bennett, W.L. (1998) 'The Uncivic Culture: Communication, Identity, and the Rise of Lifestyle Politics', *PS Political Science and Politics*, 31(4), 741–762.

Berinsky, A.J. (1999) 'The Two Faces of Public Opinion', *American Journal of Political Science*, 43(4), 1209–1230.

Bollen, J., H. Mao and X. Zeng (2011) 'Twitter Mood Predicts the Stock Market', *Journal of Computational Science*, 2(1), 1–8.

Bollen, J., A. Pepe and H. Mao (2009) 'Modeling Public Mood and Emotion: Twitter Sentiment and Socio-economic Phenomena', in Proceedings of the Fifth International AAAI Conference on Weblogs and Social Media (ICWSM 2011), 17–21 July 2011, Barcelona, Spain.

Brady, H.E. (2000) 'Contributions of Survey Research to Political Science', *PS: Political Science and Politics*, 33(1), 47–57.

Bratton, M. and R. Mattes (2001) 'Support for Democracy in Africa: Intrinsic or Instrumental?', *British Journal of Political Science*, 31(3), 447–474.

Briefing: The Future of Jobs, *The Economist*, 18–24 January 2014, 18–21.

Brown, N.J. (2013) 'Egypt's Failed Transition', *Journal of Democracy*, 24(4), 45–58.

Carey, J.W. (1995) 'The Press, Public Opinion, and Public Discourse', in T.L. Glasser and C.T. Salmon (eds.) *Public Opinion and the Communication of Consent* (New York: The Guilford Press).

Carothers, T. (2002) 'The End of the Transition Paradigm', *Journal of Democracy*, 13(1), 5–21.

Castells, M. (2008) 'The New Public Sphere: Global Civil Society, Communication Networks and Global Governance', *The Annals of the American Academy of Political and Social Science*, 616, 78–94.

——(2012) *Networks of Outrage and Hope. Social Movements in the Internet Age* (Cambridge, UK: Polity Press).

Chang, J., J.W. Lee, Y. Kim and B. Zhang (2002) *Topic Extraction from Text Documents Using Multiple-Cause Networks*. School of Computer Science and Engineering, Seoul National University.

Clemens, R. (2012) 'Twitter as a Public Sphere?', *21st Century Scholar*, http://21stcenturyscholar.org/2012/06/05/twitter-as-a-public-sphere/, date accessed 20/08/2012.

DOI: 10.1057/9781137496195.0011

CNN (2012) *CNN ORC Poll,* http://i2.cdn.turner.com/cnn/2012/ images/09/10/rel10a.pdf, date accessed 18/09/2012.

CommGAP (2012) *The Public Sphere.* Communication for Governance & Accountability Program, The World Bank, http://siteresources. worldbank.org/EXTGOVACC/Resources/ PubSphereweb.pdf, date accessed 20/08/2012.

Cowen, T. (2013) *Average Is Over. Powering America beyond the Age of the Great Stagnation* (New York: Penguin).

Dahl, R.A. (1971) *Polyarchy. Participation and Opposition* (New Haven, CT: Yale University Press).

Dahl, R.A. and E.R. Tufte (1973) *Size and Democracy* (Stanford, CA: Stanford University Press).

Dahlberg, L. (2001) 'The Internet and Democratic Discourse: Exploring the Prospects of Online Deliberative Forums Extending the Public Sphere', *Information, Communication & Society,* 4(4), 615–633.

Darby, J. and R. Mac Ginty (eds.) (2008) *Contemporary Peacemaking. Conflict, Peace Processes and Post-War Reconstruction,* second edn. (Basingstoke: Palgrave Macmillan).

DataSift (2012) *Unlock Trends from Public Tweets,* http://datasift.com/ historics/, date accessed 31/07/2012.

De Jager, N. and P. du Toit (eds.) (2013) *Friend or Foe?, Dominant Party Systems in Southern Africa. Insights from the Developing World* (Claremont: UCT Press; and Tokyo: United Nations University Press).

Deibert, R. and R. Rohozinski (2010) 'Liberation vs. Control: The Future of Cyberspace', *Journal of Democracy,* 21(4), 43–57.

Democracy Barometer (2014) *Welcome Page,* http://www. democracybarometer.org/, date accessed 23/01/2014.

Diakopoulos, N.A. and D.A. Shamma (2010) *Characterizing Debate Performance via Aggregated Twitter Sentiment,* in CHI 2010: Proceedings of the 28th International Conference on Human Factors in Computing Systems, 1195–1198.

Diamond, L. (1996) 'Is the Third Wave Over?', *Journal of Democracy,* 7(3), 20–37.

——(1999) *Developing Democracy: Toward Consolidation* (Maryland: John Hopkins University Press).

——(2002) 'Elections without Democracy: Thinking about Hybrid Regimes', *Journal of Democracy,* 13(2), 21–35.

——(2010) 'Liberation Technology', *Journal of Democracy,* 21(3), 69–83.

DOI: 10.1057/9781137496195.0011

Dikötter, F. (2013) *The Tragedy of Liberation. A History of the Chinese Revolution, 1945–57* (London: Bloomsbury).

Downey, J. and N. Fenton (2003) 'New Media, Counter Publicity and the Public Sphere', *New Media & Society*, 5(2), 185–202.

Duckitt, J. (2003) 'Prejudice and Intergroup Hostility' in D.O. Sears, L. Huddy and R. Jervis (eds.) *Oxford Handbook of Political Psychology* (New York: Oxford University Press).

Eckstein, H. (1966) *Division and Cohesion in Democracy: A Study of Norway* (Princeton, NJ: Princeton University Press).

The Economist, 22–28 October 2011.

Elections.Twitter (2012) *The Twitter Political Index*, https://election.twitter.com/, date accessed 18/09/2012.

European Commission (2014) *Eurobarometer*, http://ec.europa.eu/public_opinion/index_en.htm, date accessed 23/01/2014.

Fails, M.D. and H.N. Pierce (2010) 'Changing Mass Attitudes and Democratic Deepening', *Political Research Quarterly*, 63(1), 174–187.

Finer, S.E. (1997a) *The History of Government from the Earliest Times, Vol. I, Ancient Monarchies and Empires* (Oxford: Oxford University Press).

——(1997b) *The History of Government from the Earliest Times. Vol. II: The Intermediate Ages* (New York: Oxford University Press).

Fuchs, D. (2007) 'The Political Culture Paradigm', in R.J. Dalton and H.-D. Klingeman (eds.). *The Oxford Handbook of Political Behavior* (New York: Oxford University Press).

Fukuyama, F. (1989) 'The End of History', *The National Interest*, 16, 3–18.

Gale, W., K.W. Church and D. Yarowsky (1992) 'Estimating Upper and Lower Bounds on the Performance of Word-Sense Disambiguation Programs', in Proceedings of the 30th Annual Meeting on Association for Computational Linguistics (ACL '92). Association for Computational Linguistics, Stroudsburg, PA, USA, 249–256.

Garnham, N. (1992) 'The Media and the Public Sphere', in Calhoun, C. (ed.). *Habermas and the Public Sphere* (Cambridge, MA: MIT Press).

Gat, A. (2006) *War in Human Civilization* (Oxford: Oxford University Press).

Gayo-Avello, D. (2012) ' "I Wanted to Predict Elections with Twitter and All I Got Was this Lousy Paper": A Balanced Survey on Election Prediction Using Twitter Data' (Computers and Society. Cornell University Computer Science Paper).

The GDELT Project, 2014. Watching Our World Unfold, http://gdeltproject.org/, date accessed 09/07/2014.

DOI: 10.1057/9781137496195.0011

Gieber, W. (1955) 'Do Newspapers Overplay "Negative" News?', *Journalism & Mass Communication Quarterly*, 32(September), 311–318.

Ginsberg, B. (1986) *The Captive Public: How Mass Opinion Promotes State Power* (New York: Basic Books).

Greenfield, S. (2009) *Id. The Quest for Meaning in the 21st Century* (London: Hodder & Stoughton).

Gruicic, M.D. (2011) *Internet and the Structural Transformation of Public Debate – A Comparison of the Online and Offline Public Spheres in Croatia* (master's thesis. Central European University).

Habermas, J. (1976) *Legitimation Crisis* (London: Heinemann).

——(1989) *The Structural Transformation of the Public Sphere: An Inquiry into a Category of Bourgeois Society* (Cambridge: Polity).

——(1992) *Between Fact and Norms* (Cambridge, MA: MIT Press).

Hadenius, A. and J. Teorell (2006) 'Cultural and Economic Prerequisites of Democracy: Reassessing Recent Evidence', *Studies in Comparative International Development*, 39(4), 87–106.

Halman, L. (2007) 'Political Values', in R.J. Dalton and H.-D. Klingeman (eds.). *The Oxford Handbook of Political Behavior* (New York: Oxford University Press).

Hardin, C. (1968) 'The Tragedy of the Commons', *Science*, 162.

Harris, P. and B. Reilly (eds.) (1998) *Democracy and Deep-Rooted Conflict: Options for Negotiators* (Stockholm: International Idea).

Hassner, P. (2008) 'Russia's Transition to Autocracy', *Journal of Democracy*, 19(2), 5–15.

Hauth, A. (2010) 'Twitter as a Public Sphere', *New Media and Democracy*, http://www.personal.psu.edu/alh5147/blogs/cas497a/2010/02/twitter-as-a-public-sphere.html, date accessed 20/08/2012.

Hoffer, E. (1951/1966) *The True Believer* (New York: Harper & Row, 1966 edn. also by Harper & Row).

Hopkins, D.G. and G. King (2009) 'Replication Data for a Method of Automated Nonparametric Content Analysis for Social Science', U NF:3:xlE5stLgKvpeMvxzlLxzEQ==hdl:1902.1/12898, date accessed 22/02/2012.

——(2010) 'A Method of Automated Nonparametric Content Analysis for Social Science', *American Journal of Political Science*, 54(1), 229–247.

Horowitz, D.L. (1985) *Ethnic Groups in Conflict* (Berkeley, CA: University of California Press).

——(1991) 'Anti-Modernization, National Character and Social Structure', *Journal of Contemporary History*, 26(3/4), 355–367.

DOI: 10.1057/9781137496195.0011

Howard, P.N. and M. Hussain (2011) 'The Role of the Digital Media', *Journal of Democracy*, 22(3), 35–48.

Huddy, L. (2003) 'Group Identity and Social Cohesion', in D.O. Sears, L. Huddy and R. Jervis (eds.). *Oxford Handbook of Political Psychology* (New York: Oxford University Press).

Hughes, J.J. (2008) 'Millennial Tendencies in Responses to Apocalyptic Threats', in N. Bostrom and M.M. Cirkovic (eds.). *Global Catastrophic Risks* (Oxford: Oxford University Press).

Huntington, S.P. (1988) 'One Soul at a Time: Political Science and Political Reform', *American Political Science Review*, 82(1), 3–10.

——(1991) *The Third Wave. Democratization in the Late Twentieth Century* (Norman: Oklahoma University Press).

Inglehart, R. (2003) 'How Solid Is Mass Support for Democracy: And How Can We Measure It', *Asian Barometer*, http://www.asianbarometer. org/newenglish/publications/ ConferencePapers/2003conference/ T_03_no.11.pdf, date accessed 30/05/2012.

——(2007) 'Postmaterialist Values and the Shift from Survival to Self-Expression Values', in R.J. Dalton and H.-D. Klingeman (eds.). *The Oxford Handbook of Political Behavior* (Oxford: Oxford University Press), pp. 223–239.

Inglehart, R. and C. Welzel (2005) *Modernization, Cultural Change and Democracy: The Human Development Sequence* (Cambridge: Cambridge University Press).

Knutsen, C.H. (2010) 'Measuring Effective Democracy', *International Political Science Review*, 31(2), 109–128.

Kobar (2014) *The Korea Barometer*, http://www.koreabarometer.org/, date accessed 23/01/2014.

Kornhauser, W. (1960) *The Politics of Mass Society* (London: Routledge and Kegan Paul).

Kruger, J. and D. Dunning (1999) 'Unskilled and Unaware of It: How Difficulties in Recognizing One's Own Incompetence Lead to Inflated Self-Assessments', *Journal of Personality and Social Psychology*, 77(6), 1121–1134.

Kumar, A.K.M. and A. Suresha (2010) 'An Empirical Approach for Opinion Detection Using Significant Sentences', *International Journal of Advanced Engineering & Application*, 6335(2010), 486–497.

LatinoBarometer (2012) *Online Results Analysis*, http://www. latinobarometro.org/latino/LATAnalizeQuestion.jsp, date accessed 16/08/2012.

DOI: 10.1057/9781137496195.0011

Lerner, D. (1958) *The Passing of Traditional Society: Modernization in the Middle East* (New York: Free Press).

Levitsky, S. and L. Way (2002) 'The Rise of Competitive Authoritarianism', *Journal of Democracy*, 13(2), 51–65.

Lijphart, A. (1985) *Democracies* (New Haven, CT: Yale University Press).

——(1990) *Democracies: Patterns of Majoritarian and Consensus Government in 22 Countries* (New Haven, CT: Yale University Press).

Lindsay, R. (2008) *Predicting Polls with Lexicon*, http://languagewrong. tumblr.com/post/ 55722687/predicting-polls-with-lexicon, date accessed 25/07/2012.

Linz, J.J. (1990) 'Transitions to Democracy', *Washington Quarterly*, 13, 143–62.

——(2000) *Totalitarian and Authoritarian Regimes* (Boulder, CO: Lynne Rienner Press).

Lipset, S.M. (1959/1981) *Political Man. The Social Bases of Politics* (Baltimore, MD: Johns Hopkins University Press).

Lohr, S. (2012) 'The Age of Big Data', *The New York Times*, http://www. nytimes.com/, date accessed 2/12/2012.

MacKinnon, R. (2011) 'China's "Networked Authoritarianism"', *Journal of Democracy*, 22(2), 32–46.

Masoud, T. (2011) 'The Road to (and from) Liberation Square', *Journal of Democracy*, 22(3), 20–34.

McGonigal, J. (2011) *Reality Is Broken. Why Games Make Us Better, and How they Can Change the World* (London: Jonathan Cape).

Miall, H., O. Ramsbotham and T. Woodhouse (2011) *Contemporary Conflict Resolution* (Cambridge: Polity Press, third edn.).

Moller, J. and S.-E. Skaaning (2013) 'The Third Wave: Inside the Numbers', *Journal of Democracy*, 24(4), 97–109.

Morozov, E. (2011) 'Whither Internet Control?', *Journal of Democracy*, 22(2), 62–74.

Murray, C. (2013) *Coming Apart. The State of White America, 1960–2010* (New York: Crown Forum/Random House).

Nagal, M. (2010) 'A Mathematical Model of Democratic Elections', *Current Research Journal of Social Sciences*, 2(4), 255–261.

NCCR Democracy (2014) *Democracy Barometer*, http://www. nccr-democracy.uzh.ch/ research/module5/barometer/democracy-barometer-for-established-democracies, date accessed 23/01/2014.

Neal, C. (2012) 'The Public Sphere and the New Media', *Social Media Today*, http://socialmediatoday.com/

DOI: 10.1057/9781137496195.0011

node/495708&utm_source=feedburner_twitter&utm_medium=
twitter&utm_campaign=autotweets, date accessed 20/08/2012.

Norris, P. (1996) 'Does Television Erode Social Capital? A Reply to
Putnam', *PS Political Science and Politics*, 29, 474–479.

O'Connor, B., R. Balasubramanyan, B. Routledge and N. Smith
(2010) 'From Tweets to Polls: Linking Text Sentiment to Public
Opinion Time Series', in Proceedings of ICWSM, Carnegie Mellon
University.

Olson, M. Jr. (1965) *The Logic of Collective Action. Public Goods and the
Theory of Groups* (Cambridge, MA: Harvard University Press).

Pang, B. and L. Lee (2008) 'Opinion Mining and Sentiment Analysis',
Foundations and Trends in Information Retrieval, 2(1–2), 1–135.

Pang, B., B. Lee and S. Vaithyanathan (2002) *Thumbs Up?* Sentiment
Classification Using Machine Learning Techniques. Proceedings of
EMNLP, 79–86.

Papacharissi, Z.A. (2009) 'The Virtual Sphere 2.0: The Internet, the
Public Sphere and Beyond', in Chadwick, A. and P. Howard (eds.).
Handbook of Internet Politics (Oxon: Routledge).

—— (2010) *A Private Sphere: Democracy in a Digital Age* (Cambridge:
Polity Press).

—— (2002) 'The Virtual Sphere: The Internet as a Public Sphere', *New
Media & Society*, 4(1), 9–27.

Partington, A. (ed.) (1996) *The Oxford Dictionary of Quotations*, revised
fourth edn. (Oxford: Oxford University Press).

Pettigrew, T.F. (2006) 'Intergroup Contact Theory', *Annual Review of
Psychology*, 49, 65–85.

Pettigrew, T.F. and L.R. Tropp (2006) 'A Meta-Analytic Test of
Intergroup Contact Theory', *Journal of Personality and Social
Psychology*, 90(5), 751–783.

Pinker, S. (2011) *The Better Angels of Our Nature. The Decline of Violence in
History and Its Causes* (London: Penguin).

PROCESSQ (2014) at http://ekisto.sq.ro, accessed on 25/09/2014.

Putnam, R.D. (1995) 'Turning in, Tuning out: The Strange
Disappearance of Social Capital in America', *PS Political Science &
Politics*, 28(4), 664–683.

—— (2000) *Bowling Alone. The Collapse and Revival of American
Community* (New York: Simon & Schuster).

Qiang, X. (2011) 'The Battle for the Chinese Internet', *Journal of
Democracy*, 22(2), 47–61.

DOI: 10.1057/9781137496195.0011

Rabushka, A. and K.A. Shepsle (1972) *Politics in Plural Societies. A Theory of Democratic Instability* (Columbus, OH: Charles E. Merrill).

Real Clear Politics (2012) *General Election: Romney vs. Obama*, http://www.realclearpolitics.com/epolls/2012/president/us/general_election_romney_vs_obama-1171.html, date accessed 18/09/2012.

RH Reality Check (2012) About Us. *RH Reality Check*, http://www.rhrealitycheck.org/about-us, date accessed 09/13/2012.

Ritterman J., M. Osborne and E. Klein (2009) 'Using Prediction Markets and Twitter to Predict a Swine Flu Pandemic', Publication by University of Edinburgh, http://homepages.inf.ed.ac.uk/miles/papers/swine09.pdf, date accessed 09/08/2012.

Rose, R. (2001) 'A Divergent Europe', *Journal of Democracy*, 12(1), 93–106.

Rose, R., W. Mishler and C. Haerpfer (1998) *Democracy and Its Alternatives* (Baltimore, MD: The Johns Hopkins University Press).

Sabetti, F. (2007) 'Democracy and Civic Culture', in C. Boix and S.C. Stokes (eds.). *The Oxford Handbook of Comparative Politics* (New York: Oxford University Press), pp. 340–362.

Sander, T.H. and R.D. Putnam (2010) 'Still Bowling Alone? The Post-9/11 Split', *Journal of Democracy*, 21(1), 9–16.

Sassen, S. (2006) *Territory, Authority, Rights: From Medieval to Global Assemblages* (Princeton, NJ: Princeton University Press).

Schmidt, E. and J. Cohen (2013) *The New Digital Age. Reshaping the Future of People, Nations and Business* (New York: Alfred A. Knopf).

Schmitter, P.C. (1994) 'The Proto-Science of Consolidology: Can It Improve the Outcome of Contemporary Efforts at Democratization?', *Politikon, South African Journal of Political Studies*, 21(3), 15–27.

Schneier, B. (2013) 'The Battle for Power on the Internet', https://www.schneier.co./blog/archives/2013/10/the_battle_for_1.html, date accessed 2013/11/04.

Schraeder, P.J. and H. Redissi (2011) 'Ben Ali's Fall', *Journal of Democracy*, 22(3), 5–19.

Shils, E. (1991) 'The Virtue of Civil Society', *Government and Opposition*, 26, 3–20.

Shin, D.C. (2006) *Democratization: Perspectives from Global Citizenries*, CSD Working Papers. Centre for the Study of Democracy, UC Irvine.

——(2007) 'Democratization: Perspectives from Global Citizenries' in R.J. Dalton and H.-D. Klingeman (eds.), *The Oxford Handbook of Political Behavior* (New York: Oxford University Press), pp. 259–282.

DOI: 10.1057/9781137496195.0011

Sisk, T.D. (1994) 'Perspectives of South Africa's Transition: Implications for Democratic Consolidation', *Politikon: South African Journal of Political Studies*, 21(1), 66–75.

Sluis, E. (2009) 'Twitter: Public Space or Public Sphere?', *Masters of Media*, http://mastersofmedia.hum.uva.nl/2009/10/06/twitter-public-space-or-public-sphere/, date accessed 20/08/2012.

Smith, T.W. (1987) 'Book Review: The Captive Public: How Mass Opinion Promotes State Power', *American Journal of Sociology*, 93(2), 520–522.

Spencer, R.W. (2013) 'Work Is Not a Game', *Research Technology Management*, 56(6), 59–60.

Stolle, D. (2007) 'Social Capital', in R.J. Dalton and H.-D. Klingeman (eds.). *The Oxford Handbook of Political Behavior* (New York: Oxford University Press).

Thomassen, J. (2007) 'Democratic Values', in R.J. Dalton and H.-D. Klingeman (eds.). *The Oxford Handbook of Political Behavior* (New York: Oxford University Press).

Tiun, S., R. Abdullah and T.E. Kong (2001) 'Automatic Topic Identification Using Ontology Hierarchy', *Computational Linguistics and Intelligent Text Processing*, 2004(2001), 444–453.

Trenz, H. (2009) *Digital Media and the Return of the Representative Public Sphere* (Working Paper. Centre for European Studies).

Tumasjan, A., T.O. Sprenger, G. Sandner and I.M. Welpe (2010) *Predicting Elections with Twitter: What 140 Characters Reveal about Political Sentiment* (Proceedings of the Fourth International AAAI Conference on Weblogs and Social Media. Technische Universität München).

Twitter Developers (2012) *The Streaming APIs*, https://dev.twitter.com/docs/streaming-apis, date accessed 31/07/2012.

University of Strathclyde Glasgow (2014) *New Russia Barometer*, http://www.cspp.strath.ac.uk/catalog1_0.html, date accessed 23/01/2014.

Van Beek, U. (2012) 'The Crisis that Shook the World', in U. Van Beek and E. Wnuk-Lipinski (eds.). *Democracy under Stress: The Global Crisis and Beyond* (Berlin: Barbara Budrich Publishers).

VentureBeat (2012) 'Jack Dorsey: Twitter Seeing 3 to 5 Percent Engagement on Promoted Tweets and Trends', *Venture Beat News*, http://venturebeat.com/2012/01/22/jack-dorsey-promoted-products/#vGidIvFfak4DDYXQ.99, date accessed 30/01/2012.

DOI: 10.1057/9781137496195.0011

Verba, S. (1996) 'The Citizen as Respondent: Sample Surveys and American Democracy Presidential Address, American Political Science Association, 1995', *American Political Science Review*, 90(1), 1–7.

Voice of the People (2012) *An Annual Worldwide Survey – The Voice of the People*, http://www.voice-of-the-people.net/, date accessed 16/08/2012.

WEF (2012) *Big Data, Big Impact: New Possibilities for International Development*. World Economic Forum: Vital Wave Consulting, http://www3.weforum.org/docs.

Welzel, C. and R. Inglehart (2008) 'The Role of Ordinary People in Democratization', *Journal of Democracy*, 19(1), 126–140.

WVS (2012) *World Values Survey: The World's Most Comprehensive Investigation of Political and Sociocultural Change*, http://www.worldvaluessurvey.org/, date accessed 17/06/2014.

Yay Yonamine (2013) *Using GDELT to Forecast Violence in Afghanistan*, http://jayyonamine.com/?p=645, date accessed 09/07/2014.

Yi, J., T. Nasukawa, R. Bunescu and W. Niblack (2003) *Sentiment Analyzer: Extracting Sentiments about a Given Topic Using Natural Language Processing Techniques*. IEEE International Conference on Data Mining (ICDM): 427–434.

Zakaria, F. (1997) 'The Rise of Illiberal Democracy', *Foreign Affairs*, November/December, 22–43.

Zeleny, J. (2012) 'Poll: Obama Holds Narrow Edge over Romney', *The New York Times*, http://thecaucus.blogs.nytimes.com/2012/09/14/poll-obama-holds-narrow-edge-over-romney/, date accessed 18/09/2012.

DOI: 10.1057/9781137496195.0011

Index

AfroBarometer, 41, 46–7
Age of Modernity, 13
Albrecht, K., 118–19
Allport, G., 16
Almond, G. A., 15, 17–18, 21, 27, 39
Anderson, B., 4, 18–19
Anyone, 107–9, 113
Arab Spring, 2, 9, 50, 94, 102
Arendt, H., 21, 51
atomisation, 22–3
automated content analysis, 4–5, 7
automated non-parametric content analysis, 55–6
automated topic extraction, 86–8
autonomy, 98, 117

Ben Ali, Z. A., 94
Bennett, W. L., 29–31, 114
Beta Signup trial, 66
Big Data, 4, 6, 53–4
Bollen, J., 55
BrandsEye, 65
capitalism, 22, 28, 32, 97–8

Carey, J. W., 52
Carothers, T., 27
Castells, M., 52, 97–8, 102, 117
China, 13, 110
Chinese Communist Revolution, 23, 110–12
citizen/citizens

and Civic Culture, 15–17
democratic, 17, 116, 119
global, 6
Greek, 14
citizen effectiveness, 7, 13–14
political cohesion and, 17–21
and political culture, 15
social cohesion and, 15–17
Civic Culture
and political identity, 17–18
and role of citizens, 15–17
and survey data in the UK and US, 16–17
The Civic Culture. Political Attitudes and Democracy in Five Nations, 15, 27
civil society, 16–17, 21–2, 27–8, 30
Cohen, J., 96–7, 119
Collecta, 69
collective identity, 18, 23, 30, 107–9
communism, 25, 31
computer games, 105–8, 110, 112–16
counter-public spheres, 52–3
Cowen, T., 115–17
CrowdEye, 69

Dahl, R., 7
data processing platforms, 65–6
collection and processing of Tweets, 66–70

DOI: 10.1057/9781137496195.0012

DOI: 10.1057/9781137496195.0012

DOI: 10.1057/9781137496195.0012

GPSR Compliance
The European Union's (EU) General Product Safety Regulation (GPSR) is a set
of rules that requires consumer products to be safe and our obligations to
ensure this.

If you have any concerns about our products, you can contact us on

ProductSafety@springernature.com

In case Publisher is established outside the EU, the EU authorized
representative is:

Springer Nature Customer Service Center GmbH
Europaplatz 3
69115 Heidelberg, Germany